1975

# The
# School
# Prayer
# Decisions

From Court Policy
to Local Practice

Kenneth M. Dolbeare
and
Phillip E. Hammond

The University of Chicago Press
Chicago and London

International Standard Book Number: 0-226-15515-3
Library of Congress Catalog Card Number: 70-140461

**The University of Chicago Press, Chicago 60637**
**The University of Chicago Press, Ltd., London**

© 1971 by The University of Chicago
All rights reserved. Published 1971

Printed in the United States of America

**For Patricia
and Timothy,
Jared
and Dana**

# Contents

# Preface

Had circumstances been different, this would have been a
report on only four carefully selected communities and how
they responded to certain rulings of the United States
Supreme Court. The original impetus had been our interest
in public opinion and the Supreme Court—what difference
it makes that the Court's decisions are received by some
who approve and others who disapprove of the Court and its
products. We had decided to focus on the impress of public
opinion in the "school prayers" issue, doing so in the
midwestern state we call Midway, and we designed a
comparative framework for our inquiry. In 1968 we
therefore sought four Midway communities according to
two criteria: (1) Had their school districts complied with
the Court rulings of 1962 and 1963, or were they resisting
Court directives by continuing to recite prayers or read
from the Bible? This information we had from mail
questionnaires returned by school superintendents. (2)
Whether they complied or not, did these communities
experience considerable public interest in the matter of
schoolhouse religion, or was there little or no public concern?

A first source of information was three correspondents in each town; the second was to be a review of the towns' newspapers since the 1962 decision. Our design called for one community of each of the resulting four types, and if, for comparability, we had to settle for reasonably small (5,000–10,000 population) towns, at least we were able to select places that boasted daily newspapers and were county seats and marketing centers.

But we discovered that despite mail testimony from the school superintendent, the newspaper editor, and one or another clergyman, we could ourselves document absolutely no public interest in schoolhouse religion in any of the four selected sites. A review of their daily newspapers, for example, revealed no public outcry whatsoever. Moreover, neither did the two ostensibly "complying" school districts differ from the two admittedly noncomplying districts, a fact all too obvious once we had completed first-round interviews in each town. Almost every imaginable school religious practice seemingly existed in every community—and with no public concern.

It became disconcertingly clear that we could not research the role of public opinion in compliance with a Supreme Court edict if there was neither compliance with, nor public opinion about, the edict. Adapting our research design to local reality, we added another, purposely larger, community and interviewed extensively at state levels in both governmental and private agencies. No longer able to inquire into public opinion and compliance with Supreme Court decisions, we began to ask how failure to comply was so prevalent and so easy to maintain with impunity.

The report that follows, therefore, reflects research that changed strategies, leading to a fruitful, if different, analysis of American sociopolitical life. How can decisions be rendered at the national level and be without effect at the local level? What factors determine the reception given by a local government to a policy handed to it from above? How can the interpretations of the United States Supreme Court, the highest law of the land, be systematically controverted? These are but some of the questions forced upon us by the circumstances of our research. If, instead of neat categories of *compliance* and *resistance* to Supreme Court decisions, we therefore are forced to talk of the variety of *responses,* especially as they are formed by state and local factors, our defense is that such a story illuminates more of the reality of our society than the story we had set out to tell of those four carefully selected towns.

The size of this book is no measure of the number of organizations and individuals who contributed to the research involved. The primary sponsor was the Walter E. Meyer Research Institute of Law, a grant from which made possible the field study portion of the project. The Graduate Research Committee assisted in earlier survey stages by a grant of funds made available by the Wisconsin Alumni Research Foundation. Professor Wilbur Katz of the University of Wisconsin Law School gave freely of his time and expertise as consultant and adviser throughout. Professors R. B. Dierenfield of Macalester College and Donald Reich of Oberlin College very kindly made available data which they collected, and we are very appreciative of their generosity. We were fortunate to have as interviewers Brian Aldrich, Richard Bunce, Michael Kirn, Jon Lampman, and Robert Distefano, all graduate students in political science or sociology at the University of Wisconsin. Earlier survey work profited from the assistance of Sheila Brigham, Douglas Gurak, Dede Noll, and Eric Schulenberg. We are particularly grateful to Eleanor Perlmutter, Carolyn Shettle, and Paul Swain, graduate students at the University of Wisconsin, for permitting us to draw upon data which they independently collected for masters' theses under one or the other of the authors. We have also profited from the constructive criticism of several of our colleagues on early drafts of portions of this manuscript. And certainly not least, we want to express our gratitude also to the many officials and citizens of Midway who gave freely of their time to educate us in the political realities of their situations. All of these people have contributed wholeheartedly; any omissions of fact or errors of interpretation are the responsibility of the authors.

We have included an appendix describing our research premises and methodology in some detail, in order that our approach and interpretations may be examined more closely.

# Part One

# The Context of Inquiry

# 1  The Law of the Land

Myth and Reality

Even in tranquil times, the United States government annually generates numbers of new laws, regulations, and decisions which require citizens to modify their behavior in important ways. In the past decade, some sweeping changes were mandated by congressional statutes, presidential orders, and Supreme Court decisions. Dramatic newspaper headlines follow every major action of this kind. Commentators speculate profoundly on their significance and implications. Politicians, corporations, interest groups, and powerful individuals struggle determinedly over specific details of draftsmanship, appropriations, and implementation. Citizens react with enthusiasm, denunciation, or indifference, according to their perceptions and preferences.

But there is often a great gap between the official legal requirement and the actual experience of citizens' lives. Though things *appear* to change, they *actually* remain the same. Noble ideals are emblazoned on the statute books in Washington—promising much, but often providing little, to the ordinary citizen. We are all aware of this gap, at least in the abstract. Illustrations readily spring to mind. Racial discrimination alone, recently the subect of so much national rule-making, provides hundreds of examples every day. It is the gap between rhetoric and reality, symbol and substance[1], and the gap exacerbates already strained social and political relationships.

That such a gap exists is all too clear, but its incidence, causes, and implications are not. We know little of a systematic or comprehensive nature about the impact of national rule-making; frequently, not even the people supposed to be affected by new legislation are aware of its actual consequences. Some research has been directed at the administrative processes by which national policies are implemented,[2] but little at the social and political barriers which absorb or deflect change-inducing national requirements before they reach the local behavioral level.[3]

The implications of the rhetoric-reality gap are often the subject of confident assertions, but of quite contrasting kinds. To some the gap is the inevitable product of man's incapacity to conform the real world to his high ideals. To others it is a functional means whereby political brokers can preserve the fragile accommodations that hold the society together. To others it is an illustration of a cynical carrot-and-stick process by which powerful elites manage deprived masses. To still others it is a source of mass apathy or alienation. No doubt it is all of these in some combination in most real-life situations. But we do not really know, because evidence has not often been brought to bear on the effects of specific and perceived "gaps" on popular attitudes and behavior.

1. Murray Edelman's *The Symbolic Uses of Politics* (Urbana: University of Illinois Press, 1964) contains a number of suggestions along these lines.

2. Many of these works are synthesized in Harold L. Wilensky, *Organizational Intelligence* (New York: Basic Books, Inc., 1967). An excellent bibliography appears on pp. 193–207.

3. This, despite the historic Sumnerian debate in theory over whether law can change the mores. An exception to this general statement is the large body of recent work generated by the problems of school desegregation. In part illustrative of the characterization in the next sentence of the text, this work is also a good deal broader in orientation. For major examples, see Robert Crain et al., *The Politics of School Desegregation* (Chicago: Aldine, 1967); Raymond W. Mack et al., *Desegregation and Education* (New York: Random House, 1968); and the symposium (with bibliography) in the *Law and Society Review*, vol. 2 (November, 1967).

With this general framework in mind, we have attempted a modest contribution to understanding barriers to change. As a result of several different types and levels of analysis, we have focused on the ways in which state and local leaders, bearing official responsibility for carrying out the Supreme Court's mandate regarding elimination of schoolhouse religious activities, managed to avoid taking action and to preserve the status quo of prayers and other religious observances —all without arousing controversy. If the impact of these decisions were to be measured by the extent of change in the classrooms of Midway, our anonymous Midwestern state, that impact could only be called negligible. But this means that state and local officials and others holding power were successful both in deflecting the national mandate for change and in discouraging local efforts to use that mandate to bring change about. This process of managing the Midway state and local political agendas so as to avoid conflict and preserve the status quo reveals some crucial aspects of the linkage between national action and local consequences. In short, we shall gain insight into one important component of the rhetoric-reality problem. To be sure, the subject of Supreme Court rulings on schoolhouse religion involves some unique features. But as we shall see, the principal effect of using this subject probably is to highlight the discretion of state and local leaders, thereby making possible fuller understanding of the techniques and perceptions of those leaders than would be possible in situations where their discretion is less. The link between a Court decision and the behavior of state and local leaders will be explored in more general terms in chapter 7, in the broader context of the national policy–local consequences disjunction.

## Inertia in Midway: An Overview

We shall tell the story of five Midway towns where, five years after the Court's outlawing of the practice, the schools have continued to say prayers, read from the Bible, and conduct many other forms of supposedly unconstitutional religious observances. Local leaders are not deliberately defying the Court; they have simply found it congenial and possible to continue established local practice without regard to the Court's decisions. Those who might have wanted to follow the law of the land were discouraged, isolated, or rendered impotent. School superintendents, even some who agreed with the Court's rulings, have participated in their schools' religious activities and, incidentally, soberly declared in questionnaire surveys that their schools are in full compliance with the Court mandate. Law enforcement and state educational officers with years of experience and close local contacts sincerely deny that they know of any violations of the Court's holdings. During this entire five-year period, moreover, *not a single lawsuit* challenging the ongoing practices in the schools has been initiated by *any* parent or taxpayer in the state.[4]

We think that there are four paramount reasons for this flagrant noncompliance with the Court's constitutional ruling on school prayers and Bible reading, each bearing on the larger problem of the gap between national policy and local consequences.

The first explanation is that every state and local official has what is to him a good reason for not assuming responsibility to act consistently with the Court's decision. Each public official starts, of course, with his own value preferences and sense of what he should do because of the job he holds. But he acts in a context of other people's power and preferences. Therefore he must set up priorities among his goals, expecting to submerge some in order to achieve others. In such a context, every official could be in agreement with the Court's ruling, even perceiving it as part of his job to carry it out, but still actually do nothing because doing something is simply not important enough to jeopardize his chances of getting other more crucial goals achieved. To an individual official, it may just not be worth risking loss of the higher priority items to do anything about the Supreme Court's requirement. The citizen who would like his child to be free of prayers and other people's Bibles, or who thinks that his community should abide by the law of the land, may not find this set of circumstances a very satisfying explanation. However "understandable" refusal to act may be in the case of an individual official—or all state and local government officers generally—it may be small consolation to the man in the street to find that those in authority have such "good" reasons for not complying with national policy. Yet

4. Not all trial court decisions are reported publicly in official records or local newspapers. Thus, some decision may have been made, or some suit filed and terminated without a decision on the merits; but our search revealed no such case.

such reasons do exist; they are the first factor in explaining the inertia in Midway.

The second explanation is that officials and other leaders, having tacitly committed themselves to ignoring the Court's mandate as long as possible, apparently develop perceptual screens which enable them to avoid knowledge threatening or conflicting with the accommodation they have made. In this way their inactivity and the resultant noncompliance is rationalized away. State education officials, for example, apparently can become genuinely ignorant of the practices in their schools; leaders of such concerned interest groups as the Civil Liberties Union or the Council of Churches may acquire the same blinders. In another manifestation, responsible officials at all levels begin to misinterpret the requirements of the Court's ruling: they see it as outlawing only state-prescribed prayers or prohibiting only explicit local requirements for religious observances, and therefore as not reaching teachers' discretionary practices in the classroom. They see it as a question of voluntarism, of the right of the majority to exercise their religion. Thus superintendents of unquestioned integrity, for example, can indicate in mail questionnaire responses that their districts are in full compliance with the Court's rulings when they are actually engaging in every form of religious activity known to the American public school system.

The third major explanation, and perhaps the most important one, is that the basic operating principle of local leaders calls for the avoidance of conflict at almost any cost. In all five of the towns we studied, local power structures thoroughly permeate their communities and both subtly and openly discourage controversy of any kind. Although in most cases key members of local power structures only marginally favor schoolhouse religion on its merits, and acknowledge the abstract duty to obey the Court, they are unanimous in wanting to avoid public airing of the issue and hence are entirely committed to maintaining the status quo of religious practices. Their preference is to keep decision-making within their ranks and thus to suppress all issues that threaten such smooth-working processes. It is not even necessary for local powerful figures to give explicit instructions to school boards or superintendents; the latter know well what is expected of them and what it would cost in support for other educational goals if they failed to keep the lid on the potentially incendiary schoolhouse religion issue. Conflict avoidance, of course, when elevated to the level of a basic operating principle, not only becomes managed quiescence but can also be a far-reaching denial of democratic participation. It may come as news to some, though hardly to many, that small town governance frequently falls far short of the democratic ideal which it is so often said to embody.

Fourth, there were no regular channels through which the issue could be raised to official visibility. Neither state nor local officials could be forced to take a stand on this question through any institutionalized procedure. At the state level, relevant interest groups such as the Civil Liberties Union or the Council of Churches saw no available and economically feasible public route to put the issue onto an official agenda. At the local level, there were not even any potentially interested groups or prominent individuals who might have raised the issue of compliance. Local ministers, not very well integrated into the decision-making apparatus of their communities in any event, were further neutralized by disagreement among themselves over mechanics and by their perception of opposition from parishioners. And if the ministers did not take action on a religious issue, lay citizens were even less inclined to do so on their own initiative.

The absence of channels or arenas through which the issue might be legitimately and routinely raised means that an individual's only recourse is to initiate a lawsuit. The social and psychological costs of doing so, and the possible isolation or ostracism which might follow, make this an unlikely course in a small town setting. The procedural opportunities for challenging the acts of a public official in Midway are not as readily invoked or as effective as they are in some states, and so the overall context would be discouraging for even the most determined advocate of separation of church and state.

## Court Decisions in State and Local Context
### Some Special Circumstances

So far we have been using words like *leaders, officials, or power holders* more or less interchangeably. In place of these words we shall be using a single term, *elite,* meaning those persons who, for whatever reason, have more than the usual power or responsibility in a given context. Presently we shall discuss the matter of who constitutes the elite in educational affairs in Midway, and the state level elite will be distinguished from elites at a local level. Whether the educational elites are elites in other realms as well is a question we shall address later on, but our usage here is quite independent of the answer to that question. Our purpose, in other words, is not to prejudge the case of who rules in the state and communities of Midway but is merely to call by a single name those who in fact are found to rule.

Ours, then, is a study of the responses of state and local elites to a Supreme Court decision requiring change in their communities' practices. But such a study involves some specialized circumstances and creates related analytical needs. We must be alert, for example, to any special implications of the fact that the national mandate in this instance flows from the Court rather than the Congress or the president. It is possible, too, that the issue of schoolhouse religion engages a peculiar set of elite and public reactions and thus is very untypical. We must remember also that the setting for the study is small-town, midwestern America. Each of these facts requires some care in analysis and imposes some constraints on the scope of interpretations which may emerge. But we can adapt our inquiry to such limitations reasonably well, and make profitable use of the opportunities offered.

The fact that this national thrust toward change emanated from the Supreme Court is of course a basic structuring element in our inquiry. The phrasing of the opinion itself left some ambiguities available for exploitation by those so inclined, and no comprehensive or specific standards of conduct were prescribed. More important, no agency of the national or state governments carries responsibility for implementing Court decisions; no bureaucracy with overseeing, investigative, or enforcement responsibilities was charged with supporting the ruling. If there is to be enforcement (in the strict sense) under such circumstances, it must usually come through the lower courts. In this instance, of course, the courts would have to be invoked by local taxpayers or parents. Such courts would not be routinely involved in the subject area, as is the case in regard to the recent Supreme Court initiatives regarding the rights of defendants in criminal cases. (In the latter situations, the new rights are readily claimed by defendants at their trials and can be insisted upon by higher courts, with resulting impetus toward conformance with Supreme Court requirements.) Enforcement is rendered

even more difficult by the fact that actual implementation is
in the hands of a large number of people—the classroom
teachers of the nation, subject, we may assume, to the close
and sometimes emotional attention of some parents.
Although the mechanics of enforcement are thus distinctive, they imply no unique situation in American politics.
Behavior-changing requirements emanating from the Supreme
Court are neither new nor different in kind from those produced by the other institutions of government. Their political
character, in the sense of allocating burdens and benefits
within the society, are too evident to require comment.
Further, under the long-settled principles of American federalism, state and local officials bear responsibility for carrying
out the provisions of the United States Constitution and laws
along with their other duties. There are, in other words,
many potential agents and means for putting Court decisions
into effect, just as there are for other national mandates.
What is *really* different about the reception of all such national
policies by state and local officials, elites, and the public is
the extent to which they happen to share the goals being
fostered.

Court-initiated attempts to change local practices are actually better subjects for comparative inquiry than some other
types of national rule-making might be. In the past several
years, social scientists have examined compliance with Court
decisions in a number of ways and in a variety of contexts.[5]
When we have analyzed our findings, we shall try to integrate

---

5. Gordon Patric, "The Aftermath of a Supreme Court Decision,"
*Journal of Public Law* 6 (1957): 455–63; Frank Sorauf,
*"Zorach v. Clauson:* The Impact of a Supreme Court Decision,"
*American Political Science Review* 53 (1959): 777–91: Stephen
Wasby, "Public Law, Politics, and the Local Courts: Obscene
Literature in Portland," *Journal of Public Law* 14 (1965): 105-30;
Ellis Katz, "Patterns of Compliance with the *Schempp* Decision,"
*Journal of Public Law* 14 (1963): 396-408; William M. Beaney
and Edward N. Beiser, "Prayer and Politics: The Impact of
*Engel* and *Schempp* on the Political Process," *Journal of Public
Law* 13 (1964): 475–503; R. H. Birkby, "The Supreme Court and
the Bible: Tennessee Reactions to the *Schempp* Decision," *Midwest
Journal of Political Science* 10 (August 1966): 304-19; Richard
M. Johnson, *The Dynamics of Compliance: Supreme Court Decision-
Making from a New Perspective* (Evanston: Northwestern
University Press, 1967); Donald R. Reich, "The Impact of Judicial
Decision-Making: The School Prayer Cases," in David H. Everson,
ed., *The Supreme Court as Policy Maker: Three Studies on the
Impact of Judicial Decisions* (Carbondale, Ill.: Southern Illinois
University Press, Public Affairs Research Bureau, 1968), pp. 44–81.

them with interpretations and hypotheses emerging from this growing body of literature.

The particular setting of this inquiry is also relevant to the nature of the process we shall describe. Midwestern small towns are indeed distinctive. They normally have homogenous populations in which there are relatively few "outlanders" in a religious or ethnic sense. Most of them appear to be dominated by a relatively small group of men, or power structures, at least in our experience. And they are likely to be imbued with a Christian ethic which sees Protestant religious exercises in the public schools as a neutral posture toward religion, because it offends no one of consequence. Such towns, it may be assumed, would naturally have been resistant to the Supreme Court's ruling against prayers and Bible reading in the schools. But this is just the point—in some Midwestern states, some state officials issued rulings against religious observances; some school boards, superintendents, and principals acted to eliminate the newly unconstitutional behavior; and there were many instances of controversy, as parents and others became aroused about the issue. In Midway, however, none of these actions occurred. We seek to learn why. And in view of experience across the nation, we reject the determinist conclusion that "the people didn't want to change."

For reasons shortly to be described, we think the focus of inquiry should be on state and local elites. Let us note now that they represent a particularly crucial link, not only for our inquiry and the larger questions at which it is directed, but for the operation of the American political system generally. Their role is highlighted in our inquiry because American federalism operates in this instance to place both major responsibility and broad discretion in their hands, and because each of our small towns was so thoroughly dominated by its local power structure. And where they play such a vital role, we may hope to see characteristics of their operations which offer even more general implications. For example, we mentioned earlier that many officials saw schoolhouse religion as a low-priority issue, and therefore not something for which they wanted to spend some of their accumulated good will and political support. It should be clear that this is only part of the story. There are almost always "more important" issues for elites to take up, and the real question is whether it is possible to force any given issue onto the agenda. If it is not possible for some segments of nonelites to force an issue onto the agenda even when they do not wish to become embroiled with it, then it may be that the real agenda of politics is made up essentially of elites' preferences. Again, the implications for the process of change are profound.

In summary, we see our inquiry drawing upon the conceptual apparatus and research findings of both community power studies and judicial impact studies. It is aimed at one relatively narrow but important area of the rhetoric-reality gap, the role of state and local elites as barriers to change. Of course, the judicial origins of the change in question, and the special characteristics of setting and subject involved, impose limitations; nevertheless, they also offer opportunities.

# 2 Public Response to the Court  The Crucial Role of Local Elites

Two major streams of previous research converge to suggest strongly that local elites play the key role in determining local response to change-requiring Supreme Court decisions. One is survey research sampling of the attitudes of both general and special publics toward the Court and its decisions.[1] The other is the growing body of studies of the impact of judicial decisions, including both quantitative views of "compliance" and "noncompliance"[2] in various settings, and case studies of "compliance" in a single community or school system.[3] In this chapter, we shall briefly review the findings of both lines of research, showing (particularly through our own attitudinal research in Wisconsin) the extent to which local elites—public officials and private leaders—are crucial to shaping response to the Court.

## Attitudes toward the Court
It should come as no surprise that the public is generally very poorly informed about the decisions which the Court has made, but that the prayer and Bible reading decisons

of 1962 and 1963 were exceptionally well-known cases. Re-action varied among states, of course, and was bound up with and affected by preexisting attitudes toward the Court as an institution. Let us document each of these statements in turn.

Table 1 shows the relative prominence of school prayers among various actual and suggested (but nonexistent) subjects of Supreme Court decision-making. The data are drawn from the responses of a sample of 627 Wisconsin adults in a survey conducted by the Wisconsin Survey Research Laboratory in 1966. Very few respondents answered correctly regarding all decisions, and only 15 percent gave more than four correct answers. But 71 percent answered correctly regarding school prayers, practically the same number who were aware of the school segregation decisions. Clearly, schoolhouse religion is well recognized by the general public as an area in which the Court has acted. This is one reason why this subject is particularly well suited for an analysis of this kind: it is far from intrinsically a "back-room" issue capable of being resolved by intra-elite negotiations without public notice.

Levels of approval and disapproval of the Court's decisions varied sharply between states. For example, 55 percent of a sample of a Minnesota adult population approved and only 31 percent disapproved of *Engel,* while in Texas two years later approval of *Schempp* was expressed by only 28 percent

1. Kenneth M. Dolbeare, "The Public Views the Supreme Court," in Herbert Jacob, ed., *Law and Politics in the Federal Courts* (Boston: Little, Brown & Co., 1967); Kenneth M. Dolbeare and Phillip E. Hammond, "The Political Party Basis of Attitudes toward the U.S. Supreme Court," *Public Opinion Quarterly,* 32 (1968): 16–30; John Kessel, "Public Perceptions of the Supreme Court," *Midwest Journal of Political Science* 10 (1966): 167–191; Walter Murphy and Joseph Tanenhaus, "Public Opinion and the United States Supreme Court: A Preliminary Mapping of Some Prerequesites for Court Legitimation of Regime Changes," in Joel B. Grossman and Joseph Tanenhaus, *Frontiers of Judicial Research* (New York: John Wiley & Sons, Inc., 1969).

2. We deliberately eschew use of the dichotomy of "compliance and noncompliance," though this is the approach taken by most judicial impact studies. The variety of possible responses in the wake of a decision is so great, and the meaning of the term as used by various researchers and survey respondents so uncertain and conflicting, that we prefer to use *response* as the general term and specify precisely what kinds of response we are talking about in all particular situations.

3. See works cited in ch. 1, n. 5, above.

TABLE 1

*Relative Prominence of School-Prayer Decisions*

| Subject | Yes: Court Made Decision | No: Court Made No Decisions | Don't Know |
|---------|--------------------------|----------------------------|------------|
| Rights of defendants accused of crimes | 26% | 7% | 66% |
| Federal aid to education | 45 | 10 | 45 |
| Redistricting for state legislatures | 35 | 9 | 56 |
| Medical care for the aged | 52 | 24 | 24 |
| Prayers in public schools | 71 | 7 | 22 |
| Segregation in public schools | 72 | 7 | 21 |
| Urban renewal program | 26 | 15 | 59 |
| John Birch Society | 23 | 19 | 58 |

Question: Do you happen to recall whether the Supreme Court made a decision in recent years on —?

and disapproval by 60 percent.[4] Bound up in these reactions is a whole range of attitudes toward the Supreme Court as well as toward the issue of prayers and Bible reading in the schools. Data from Minnesota show this dramatically.

Respondents were first asked whether they favored or opposed prayer at the start of the school day and, after their answers had been recorded, were then told that the Supreme Court had ruled the practice illegal and asked whether they liked the decision or not. Table 2 shows how the Court's action blurred their policy preferences: nearly half of those favoring prayer nevertheless liked the decision! Apparently the symbolism of the Court is capable of shifting what may

4. These data are drawn from the Minnesota and Texas Polls respectively and were made available for re-analysis by the Roper Public Opinion Research Center in Williamstown, Massachusetts, for whose cooperation we are very grateful.

have been rather lightly held policy preferences for many
people.

TABLE 2

*Responses to Court Decision by Preference for Prayer*

|  | Opinion regarding use of prayer in Minnesota schools* | |
| --- | --- | --- |
|  | Favor (74%) | Oppose (26%) |
| Supreme Court has ruled against prayer—do you like the decision or dislike it?† | | |
| Like it | 44% | 89% |
| Dislike it | 44% | 4% |
| Don't care | 12% | 7% |
|  | 100% | 100% |
|  | N = 395 | N = 135 |

* Question: In the public schools of some states, the school day
is opened with a time for prayer by the children. Do you favor
or oppose having a time for prayer as part of each school day
in Minnesota's public schools?

(Favor/Oppose/No opinion/Other.)

† Question: (Asked immediately after question 1 above.) The
United States Supreme Court has ruled recently that it is not
legal to have the school board or any public official or agency
prepare one certain prayer for school children to recite in the
public schools. Do you like the Supreme Court ruling? Dislike
it? Or don't you care one way or the other?

(Like it/Dislike it/Don't care/No opinion/Other.)

Survey research findings have differed as to the bases of
public attitudes toward the Supreme Court. One major
national study found specific approval and disapproval closely
related to the Court's support for or apparent opposition to
respondents' policy preferences.[5] Our own findings indicated
that the general public was likely to approve or disapprove
of the Court's performance according to broad political party
lines, with Democrats generally showing much higher levels

5. Murphy and Tanenhaus, *"Public Opinion and the United States
Supreme Court."*

of approval.[6] The difference may be more apparent than real, however. The national study eliminated many respondents who were least informed about the Court and focused its analysis on the relatively well informed, whom we also found to evaluate the Court principally in terms of its (and their) policy preferences.

Comparison of local leaders' and the general public's knowledge and resulting evaluations of the Court emphasizes the importance of these differences.[7] Even in relatively isolated communities, leaders were much more attentive to the Court, knowledgeable about its activities, and decisive in their reactions to it. Data for leaders in Wisconsin were collected by mail questionnaire three months after the survey of Wisconsin's general public in 1966. Three groups were contacted: (1) Republican and Democratic Wisconsin county chairmen, of whom 49 percent (N = 71) responded; (2) Protestant clergymen, selected randomly from the Wisconsin lists for the Methodist, Conservative Baptist, and United Church of Christ denominations, of whom 90 percent (N = 128) responded; and (3) Wisconsin newspaper editors, selected randomly from the *Ayer Directory,* of whom 69 percent (N = 44) responded.

Table 3 shows that all three types of leaders know more about the Court's actions and assign it a larger role in governing the nation than does the general public. The first line of table 3 is the composite of answers to a battery of eight questions asking whether the Court had rendered decisions in specified areas. In four cases (school prayers, school desegregation, reapportionment, and defendants' rights) it had, and respondents were assigned one point for each correct answer. In the other four cases (federal aid to education, medical care for the aged, urban renewal, and the John Birch Society) the Court had not acted, and again one point was given for each correct answer. Scores could thus range from 0 to 8. As the table shows, knowledge of the Supreme Court is strongly related to educational level; nevertheless, each type of leader is significantly more knowledgeable about the

6. Dolbeare and Hammond, *"The Political Party Basis of Attitudes."*
7. We are indebted to Eleanor Perlmutter Simpson for her assistance in the research about to be discussed. She reported some of it in an M.A. thesis, "Leader–Non-leader Differences in Benevolence toward the Supreme Court," Department of Sociology, University of Wisconsin, 1968. Paul Swain collected other data for this comparison, and we are grateful for his assistance also.

TABLE 3

*Public and Leader Perception of the Importance of Supreme Court (Wisconsin, 1966)*

| | PUBLIC | | | | | LEADERS | | | |
| | Grade School | Some High School | High School | At Least Some College | All Public | County Chairmen | Clergy | Editors | All Leaders |
|---|---|---|---|---|---|---|---|---|---|
| Average knowledge score | 1.8 | 2.4 | 2.8 | 4.1 | 2.7 | 5.6 | 5.0 | 5.4 | 5.2 |
| Percentage saying Court can make important changes* | 59 | 61 | 83 | 79 | 71 | 89 | 91 | 90 | 91 |
| Percentage saying Court is most important branch† | 5 | 4 | 6 | 11 | 6 | 17 | 18 | 24 | 19 |
| N = | 169 | 101 | 239 | 115 | 624 | 71 | 128 | 44 | 243 |

* Question: Which one of the next statements comes closest to your own feelings? First: "The U.S. Supreme Court can make important changes in the way the average American lives." Or second: "The U.S. Supreme Court can't affect the lives of average people." (Percentage choosing first statement.)

† Question: "Of the many things which are done by the government in Washington, which branch of the government would you say does the most important things in deciding how Americans are going to live—the Congress, the Supreme Court, or the president?"

Court than even comparably educated members of the public. Among leaders, over 80 percent correctly identified the four instances where the Court *had* acted; most errors thus arose from failing to know where it had *not* acted. For example, almost half the leaders incorrectly said that federal aid to education had been on the docket.

With the public, a different pattern obtains. In every instance, their rate of correct answers is less than that of the leaders, but apart from the desegregation and school-prayer cases (for which 72 and 71 percent were correct), no decision was correctly perceived by more than 35 percent, the average being one-fifth. As might have been anticipated, the public's modal response in most instances was "Don't know."

Given such a sizable gap in knowledge levels between leaders and the public, leaders' assignment of greater importance to the Supreme Court is no surprise. More than 90 percent of the leaders assert that the Court can make important social changes, while only 71 percent of the public at large agrees. Even the most stringent test of this sentiment, as shown in the third line of table 3, reveals the same pattern: leaders are three times more likely than the public to nominate the Court as the most important of the three federal branches of government.

TABLE 4

*Approval of Court by Conservatives and Moderates Among Public and Leaders (Wisconsin, 1966)*

| | Percentage Evaluating the Court as "Very Good" and "Good" | | |
| --- | --- | --- | --- |
| | Conservatives* | Moderates* | Difference |
| Public | 46% (180) | 52% (447) | 6% |
| Leaders | 26 (97) | 80 (122) | 54 |

*Question: With respect to the things the government in Washington is doing that affect people's lives in this country, do you believe the government is doing too much, is doing just about right, or is not doing enough? (Doing too much = conservative; all others = moderate.)

Not only are leaders more aware of the Court, they are also more polarized by its substantive actions in relation to their policy preferences. Table 4 compares leader and public evaluation of the Court's performance according to their self-perceived political preferences. It might reasonably be inferred from this table that leaders' much greater knowledge of the judicial branch neither bolsters nor diminishes their approval of the Court, but simply permits their political views more strongly to influence their judgment of the Court's past activity. The public, on the other hand, though perhaps potentially able to evaluate the Court on political grounds, in fact tends to remain largely unknowledgeable about it and thus relatively undifferentiated by substantive views in their approval. This interpretation gains some confirmation in the fact that, among the least knowledgeable public (those with knowledge scores of 0–2), the correlation between Court approval and moderate-conservatism is a trivial .02, whereas among the public with a knowledge score of at least 3, the correlation is .24. Both of these figures stand in sharp contrast to the .84 correlation between these two factors in the leadership group. The public, then, may be left with little but political party affiliation as a basis for judging the Supreme Court, as we have described elsewhere.[8] Leaders, on the other hand, though their judgments obviously are related to political party affiliation, are able to base those judgments on substantive political grounds.

Quite a different pattern of relationships emerges, however, if instead of retrospective evaluation of the Supreme Court, we look at prospective evaluation. Respondents were asked: "In general, would you be likely to think the right thing had been done by the government in Washington if the action had been taken by the president? By the Congress? By the Supreme Court?" In one sense, an answer of "Yes" or "Depends" rather than "No" or "Don't know" indicates a kind of trust or benevolence toward that branch of government. By telling us that they would think the right thing had been done, or that they are willing to hold in abeyance their judgment until the thing is done, people are evidencing a trusting attitude toward the institution in question. Table 5 shows the public's and leaders' answers to these queries.

Several points are worth noting about table 5. First, from

8. Dolbeare and Hammond, "The Political Party Basis of Attitudes."

both leaders and public, the Congress enjoys the higher rate
of trust; 70 percent of the latter and 89 percent of the former
indicate either a "Yes" or "Depends" answer to the inquiry

TABLE 5

*Expressions of Trust of Three Branches of Government
(Wisconsin, 1966)*

| Branch | | Public | Leaders | Difference |
|---|---|---|---|---|
| Presidency: | Yes | 36% | 16% | |
| | Depends | 17 | 47 | |
| | Total | 53 | 63 | 10% |
| Congress: | Yes | 50 | 38 | |
| | Depends | 30 | 51 | |
| | Total | 70 | 89 | 19 |
| Supreme Court: | Yes | 28 | 32 | |
| | Depends | 13 | 35 | |
| | Total | 41 | 67 | 26 |

Question: In general, would you be likely to think the right thing
had been done by the government in Washington if the action
had been taken by the President? By the Congress? By the Supreme Court?

regarding the legislative branch. Second, leaders are less
likely to give an unqualified "Yes" response to questions
about the presidency and Congress, but this is not the case
regarding the Supreme Court. Third, when total rates are
observed, leaders, compared with the public, are slightly
more trustful of the presidency, somewhat more trustful of
Congress, and noticeably more trustful of the Court. These
patterns, incidentally, obtain even with controls for education among the public and type of leader among the other.
It would seem entirely warranted to infer that leaders express
a greater sense of trust or benevolence toward these governmental institutions, especially the Supreme Court, than does
the public.

## "Compliance" with Court Decisions

Other research in this area also hints at the vital part played by leaders and officials in community reception of Supreme Court decisions. A substantial proportion of judicial-impact studies has been devoted to schoolhouse religion cases, beginning with the released time cases of the 1940s and 1950s[9] and continuing particularly with the *Engel, Schempp,* and *Murray* cases[10] of the 1960s. Two approaches have characterized this research: one uses mail questionnaire survey techniques to produce a snapshot of reported compliance by school superintendents, school board members, or teachers in a particular area, and to measure information and preferences on the issue,[11] the other employs more detailed interviewing at the micro-level, such as a particular group of school officials in one city[12] or school officials and general public in a small rural community.[13]

Birkby found in his study of compliance patterns in Tennessee that reported school board policy changes did not correlate with such likely factors as urbanization, religious pluralism, or the socioeconomic backgrounds of school board members.[14] His data led him to see local school board members as independent decision-makers whose actions would be responsive to both their preferences for prayer and their feelings of obligation to obey the Court, and secondarily to their perceptions of public preferences. Speculating with considerable sophistication, he suggested that boards might not really have changed very much by altering their formal policies anyhow, and that they might be permitting teachers to go on with religious observances, if only to avoid controversy.

9. *Illinois ex rel. McCollum* v. *Board of Education,* 333 U.S. 203 (1948), *Zorach* v. *Clauson,* 343 U.S. 306 (1952).

10. *Engel* v. *Vitale,* 370 U.S. 421 (1962); *School District of Abington Township* v. *Schempp* and *Murray* v. *Curlett,* 374 U.S. 203 (1963).

11. Patric, "The Aftermath of a Supreme Court Decision"; Sorauf, *"Zorach* v. *Clauson";* Katz, "Patterns of Compliance"; Birkby, "The Supreme Court and the Bible"; Reich, 'The Impact of Judicial Decision-Making"; H. Frank Way, "Survey Research on Judicial Decisions: The Prayer and Bible Reading Cases," *Western Political Quarterly,* vol. 21 (June 1968).

12. William K. Muir, Jr., *Prayer in the Public Schools: Law and Attitude Change* (Chicago: University of Chicago Press, 1967).

13. Richard M. Johnson, *The Dynamics of Compliance: Supreme Court Decision-Making from a New Perspective* (Evanston: Northwestern University Press, 1967).

14. Birkby, "The Supreme Court and the Bible."

Johnson's findings also highlight the independence of key local decision-makers, in this case the local school superintendent.[15] He found that, although the entire community apparently would have preferred to continue prayers in their schools, influential persons were inclined toward compliance with the Court and provided role-induced support for the decisive actions which the superintendent took chiefly as a result of his own strongly held value preferences. With this pattern of official action and influential acquiescence, no conflict was generated despite the structure of public attitudes. These two studies in particular, and Muir's subtle exploration of the psychological intricacies of response on the part of affected school system officials and teachers,[16] suggest that local elites (school superintendents, school board members, and other leaders) are crucial to the shaping of response to the Court in this area.

We think that these findings, taken together with our own data, suggest that the Court is in effect almost exclusively an object of elite attention—that elites are more responsive to, more knowledgeable of, and more confident in the Court, and therefore more likely to be the channels by which Court-initiated policies become transformed into local practice or at least are acted upon in some way. If local elites are acquiescent, effectuation of the Court policy is more likely. If they are opposed, effectuation may be a long time in coming, perhaps not until some other elite at some other level is induced to act in support of the Court's policy. For these reasons, it seems to us that the place to begin to understand the forces shaping local consequences in this subject area is with the study of local elite behavior. But local elites are not equally free to act as they see fit in all contexts. Their discretion is greatest where there have been no state-imposed requirements or criteria applicable to the situation. In the next chapter, we shall see from an analysis of regional patterns of response to the Court's religious decisions that the Midwest is the area of fewest state-level actions and of greatest local responsibility.

15. Johnson, *The Dynamics of Compliance.*
16. Muir, *Prayer in the Public Schools.*

# 3   Patterns of Response to the Schoolhouse Religion Cases of 1962 and 1963

An interpretation of the Constitution by the nation's highest court establishes new rights for some, new obligations for others. To understand how such an abstract principle became operative within the society in the case of schoolhouse religion, we must begin with the Supreme Court's two rulings themselves, the initial shock wave they generated, and the regional patterns of response which emerged. Subsequently, we will show why we have chosen to set our inquiry in five small towns of the Midwest.

## National Policy: Two Supreme Court Decisions
The First Amendment of the United States Constitution contains two provisions regarding the relationship of church and state. Broadly stated, it prohibits governments from establishing religion (the so-called no-establishment clause) and it prohibits governments from interfering with an individual's free exercise of religion (the so-called free-exercise clause). Supreme Court rulings provide some concrete applications of these two provisions. "No-establishment" in regard to education has been interpreted to

mean that governments may not support religion through
legislation, nor provide direct assistance to religious sects, as
by grants of financial aid or provision of school classrooms
for religious instruction.[1] Indirect assistance, such as bus
transportation to parochial schools, is accepted as aid to
students rather than establishment of religion,[2] and "released
time" for religious instruction is accepted as long as it is conducted off school property.[3] The right of "free exercise" has
been held to include the right of religious persons to send
their children to their own (nonpublic) schools and to re-
fuse to salute the flag, though it has not included, for example, the freedom to engage in polygamous marriage.[4]

Because there are so many possibilities for various forms
of state assistance to religion and/or interference with the
free exercise of religion, and only a relatively small number
of Supreme Court decisions in the area, many questions of
the scope of state power remain. Since World War II, as
governments have become more active in allocating financial
assistance to education, several specific state actions have
been litigated. The Supreme Court has ruled on the constitutionality of various forms of released-time programs, bus
transportation, and other financial assistance to religious education. But none of these generated the violent reaction that
greeted the Court's decisions on school prayers and Bible
reading.

*The Opinions*

*Engel* v. *Vitale*[5] was decided in 1962. The Court held it a
violation of the no-establishment clause for the New York
State Board of Regents to compose a prayer ("Almighty
God, we acknowledge our dependence upon Thee and we
beg Thy blessings upon us, our parents, our teachers and
our country") and offer it to school boards for their discretionary use. Although to some the decision appeared to
rest on the state's having *composed* the prayer, rather than
on its having authorized school boards to require or permit

1. *Illinois ex rel. McCollum* v. *Board of Education,* 333 U.S.
203 (1948).
2. *Everson* v. *Board of Education,* 330 U.S. 1 (1947).
3. *Zorach* v. *Clauson,* 343 U.S. 306 (1952).
4. In order: *Pierce* v. *Society of Sisters,* 268 U.S. 510 (1925); *West
Virginia State Board of Education* v. *Barnett,* 319 U.S. 624 (1943);
*Reynolds* v. *United States,* 98 U.S. 145 (1879).
5. 370 U.S. 421 (1962).

its use by teachers, the crucial element for the Court was the fact that the state, through its local agencies, was engaging in a devotional practice. Consistent with this principle, the Court held in *Abington Township* v. *Schempp* and *Murray* v. *Curlett*[6] the next year that it was unconstitutional for schools to require or conduct devotional use of the Lord's Prayer or Bible reading.

All of these decisions rested on the theory that the states were in effect using their powers in support of religion and therefore violating the no-establishment clause. But confusion as to the merits of the Court's ruling was possible because one might view prayers and Bible reading in schools as the free exercise of the religious preferences of students or their parents. Thus the Court might actually appear to have ruled against freedom of religion. Such twisting of the prohibition against government's establishment of any form of worship into a prohibition of the majority's freedom to exercise their religious impulses by introducing their religious observances into public schools had no basis in the Court's opinion. It was, however, urged in dissent and may have been a real source of confusion.

*The Reaction*

Within twenty-four hours after the *Engel* decision was announced, ten Congressmen had introduced bitter attacks on the Court into the *Congressional Record,* and newspapers across the country were denouncing the ruling.[7] Such diverse religious spokesmen as Cardinal Spellman, Bishop James A. Pike, Billy Graham, and Reinhold Niebuhr all publicly regretted the decision. The annual Governors' Conference the following month endorsed a constitutional amendment to permit prayers and Bible reading. Eventually, no fewer than forty-nine such amendments were filed in the Congress. Reporting of the *Engel* opinion, while extensive, was factually sketchy and often inaccurate, so that there was not only

6. 374 U.S. 203 (1963). Both *Schempp* and *Murray* are covered in the same opinion.

7. Several sources provide extensive coverage of the unusual national reaction to these decisions and have been drawn upon in this section: Paul Blanchard, *Religion and the Schools* (Boston: Beacon Press, 1963), esp. chap. 3; William Hachten, "Journalism and the Prayer Decision," *Columbia Journalism Review,* Fall 1962, pp. 4–8; David L. Grey, *The Supreme Court and the News Media* (Evanston, Ill.: Northwestern University Press, 1968); Beaney and Beiser, "Prayer and Politics," pp. 477–85.

much publicity but also much confusion surrounding what the Court had done. Reaction is well summarized in the words of the attorney who argued the case:

Within twenty-four hours, the [1962] decision came under severe attack from many religious leaders and public officials, and some educators. Thousands of critical letters and telegrams were sent to the Supreme Court and to Congressmen. Two ex-Presidents, Herbert Hoover and Dwight D. Eisenhower, opposed the decision. President Hoover went so far as to proclaim the end of the public school system.[8]

The Court in fact received more than 5,000 letters about *Engel* v. *Vitale* in 1962, and extra copies of its New York Regents prayer decision had to be printed through March 1964. The Government Printing Office, after selling about 13,500 copies, noted that it was "the largest public demand for any one opinion that anyone can remember." The staff around the Supreme Court Building claimed that tourist interest in the '62 and '63 decisions did not noticeably decline until the fall of 1964.

Not all response was negative, of course. A number of church-related groups and journals supported the decision. Educators and their journals examined the ruling extensively, and many journals editorialized in support. By the time of the *Schempp* and *Murray* decisions, reactions had coalesced around a campaign spearheaded by Congressman Frank Becker of New York and Senator Everett Dirksen of Illinois to amend the Constitution to permit nondenominational prayers, and a countering effort was mounted by civil libertarians and some church and educational groups to sustain the Court's actions. Perhaps because they were expected, or because the lines had already been drawn, the *Schempp* and *Murray* decisions did not provoke the same uproar that *Engel* did. But together they raised the subject of school prayer to the level of a major national issue.

*Lower Court Applications*

Within a year of *Schempp,* a federal district court declared invalid an Idaho statute requiring daily reading of the Bible in all public schools of that state.[9] In 1965 a United States district court in New York ruled that student-initiated prayers were permissible, but a United States court of appeals, con-

8. Quoted in Donald E. Boles, *The Two Swords* (Ames, Iowa: Iowa State University Press, 1967), p. 74.
9. *Adams* v. *Engelking,* 232 F. Supp. 666 (1964).

cluding that "plaintiffs must content themselves with having their children say these prayers before nine or after three," reversed the decision.[10] The United States Supreme Court, by refusing to accept jurisdiction, allowed the reversal to stand. A federal district court in Michigan in 1965 allowed prayers to be said or scripture to be read in public schools, but with the provisions that such activity take place before or after the "regularly scheduled class day" and that it occur in a room other than the regular homeroom.[11] In 1967 an appellate court declared unconstitutional an Illinois school district teachers' practice of using a nondenominational prayer which mentioned God.[12]

A possible exception to the Supreme Court's clear mandate might be seen in a Florida case. In 1962 lower courts were asked to rule against not only Bible reading and prayer recitation but also sectarian baccalaureate services, religious censuses among school children, and religious tests for teacher qualification. By 1964, after the Florida Supreme Court had upheld these practices, the United States Supreme Court reversed the ruling with respect to prayer and devotional Bible reading, but dismissed the other questions "for want of properly presented federal questions."[13] While these other questions, then, might yet be regarded as legally ambiguous, public schools clearly are not to engage in devotional Bible reading or the saying of prayers as part of the regular schoolroom program.

*Regional Patterns of Response*

Before the *Engel* decision, eleven states (mostly in the West) had laws prohibiting Bible reading; eleven others (mainly in the South) had laws requiring Bible reading; and twenty-six others permitted, but did not require, the practice. In a 1960 survey, 42 percent of the school districts in the continental United States reported Bible reading, and 50 percent had some kind of homeroom devotional exercises.[14]

10. *Stein* v. *Oshinsky*, 348 F. 2d 999 (1965).
11. *Reed* v. *Van Hoven*, 237 F. Supp. 48 (1965).
12. *De Spain* v. *De Kalb County Community School District*, 384 F. 2d 836 (1967).
13. *Chamberlain* v. *Dade County, Board of Public Instruction*, 84 S. Ct. 1272 (1964).
14. R. B. Dierenfield, *Religion in American Public Schools* (Washington: Public Affairs Press, 1962). Dierenfield's report must be considered only as approximate, because of 4,000 questionnaires sent out, only 55 percent were returned.

The incidence varied sharply across the country, however, as one would expect from the different state constitutional and legislative requirements: religious observances in the schools ranged from around 10 percent in the West to more than 20 percent in the Midwest and more than 70 percent and 80 percent in the East and South respectively. In another survey made in 1964-65, elementary school teachers were asked to recall their pre–1962 practices. The results, as shown in table 6, were strikingly similar in proportions.[15]

TABLE 6

*Pre-1962 Elementary-School Religious Practices*

| Region | Teachers Having Bible Reading | Teachers Having Morning Prayers |
|--------|-------------------------------|----------------------------------|
| West | 14% | 14% |
| Midwest | 28 | 38 |
| East | 62 | 83 |
| South | 80 | 87 |

In the face of such widespread and well-established practice of religious observances in the schools, there is good reason to anticipate some noncompliance. Resistance to the desegregation requirements of *Brown* v. *Board of Education* has endured from 1954 to this day, and in the schoolhouse-religion area the Supreme Court's 1948 outlawing of released-time religious education in the school building has been widely disobeyed.[16]

In the case of the more recent prayer and Bible reading decisions, evidence is clear that school officials share the general public's mixed feelings about the Supreme Court's actions. The *Nation's Schools,* in issues soon after *Engel* v. *Vitale* and again after *Schempp,* published polls of public

15. H. Frank Way, "Survey Research on Judicial Decisions: The Prayer and Bible Reading Cases," *Western Political Quarterly,* vol. 21 (June 1968). The table is a modification of information on p. 199.

16. Erwin L. Shaver, "Weekday Religious Education Secures Its Charter and Faces a Challenge," *Religious Education* 48 (January-February, 1953): 38–43; Vivian T. Thayer, *The Attack upon the American Secular School* (Boston: Beacon Press, 1951), pp. 180–81.

school administrators in which slightly more than half (51 percent) reported disapproval of the first decision, while almost half (48 percent) indicated disapproval of the second.[17] The second poll, moreover, showed that 57 percent of these administrators favored a constitutional amendment permitting Bible reading and prayer recitation in public schools.

Teachers responded similarly. The study of elementary school teachers in 1964-65 revealed that only 35 percent agreed that "devotional services have no place in the public school."[18] In reporting their pre–1962 practices as compared with their 1964-65 practices, however, these teachers indicated that the saying of prayers had dropped from the earlier rate of 60 percent to a post-decision rate of 28 percent. Bible reading declined similarly—from 48 percent before 1962 to 22 percent in 1964-65. The author of the 1960 national survey of school districts, Professor R. B. Dierenfield of Macalester College, reported that another survey by him in 1966 showed Bible reading down to 19.5 percent and prayers down to 14 percent.

Regional variation in reported compliance is marked, however. Table 7 (a rearrangement of data gathered in the teachers' survey) contrasts, in four areas of the nation, the pre–1962 rates of reciting morning prayers in elementary classrooms with the 1964-65 rates.

Even allowing for bias introduced by a less than complete return of questionnaires and by imperfect recall, these data show sharp regional differences in compliance. The South (Deep and Border), starting with a widespread practice of saying homeroom prayers, has complied very little, reducing their practice by only 26 percent. In marked contrast, the East (Northeast and Middle Atlantic), with virtually the same widespread pre–1962 practice, has complied almost entirely (87 percent). The West (Coast and Rocky Mountain), which began with a low rate, has reduced that rate by 64 percent. And the Midwest, where about a third of the

17. *Nation's Schools,* 70 (September 1962): 101; 72 (September 1963): 43. Though these polls were based on 4 percent samples of 16,000 administrators, only 42 percent and 40 percent responded. Therefore the report rates of disapproval must be considered as only approximate.

18. Way, "Survey Research on Judicial Decisions," p. 195. The findings cited in the next two paragraphs may be found on pp. 191 and 199.

TABLE 7

*Use of Morning Prayers*

| Region | Percentage of 1712 Elementary School Teachers Using Morning Prayers | | | |
|--------|----------|---------|------------|------------------------|
|        | Pre–1962 | 1964-65 | Difference | Percentage Reduction |
| West   | 14       | 5       | – 9        | 64                     |
| Midwest| 38       | 21      | –17        | 45                     |
| East   | 83       | 11      | –72        | 87                     |
| South  | 87       | 64      | –23        | 26                     |

teachers were engaging in morning prayers, now has about half that number so engaged.[19]

In an effort to identify specific school districts which complied and those which did not, and to try to account for reasons behind such varying behavior, we resurveyed all of the school districts which had reported in Dierenfield's 1960 survey that at least some of their schools engaged in devotional exercises. Presumably, all of these districts would have been faced with the question what if any changes to make after the Court decisions of 1962 and 1963. Although the return rate from the 1100 questionnaires we sent was only 57 percent, the results in gross terms show much the

19. A number of qualifications must be kept in mind, however, when considering these figures. Aside from the fact that the survey was limited to elementary teachers, it is not clear, for example, what those teachers who had begun teaching after 1962 were doing in the way of homeroom devotionals. Moreover, the table, properly speaking, does not indicate *teacher* compliance necessarily but only the extent of *regional* compliance. That is, the data are given as rates for areas at two points in time and do not indicate individual change. For example, it is possible that half of the teachers in the region were leading devotionals but stopped as the other half began. The figures would be shown as 50 percent for both time periods, suggesting no change, when in fact there was a 100 percent change. Such an extreme example is so unlikely as to be safely ruled out, of course, but it is important to remember that the data above allow inferences only.
20. Professor R. B. Dierenfield graciously made available the data collected in his original 1960 survey, and we are indebted to him for his kind cooperation. Our resurvey was directed exclusively to those districts which had reported religious activities of some kind in 1960.

same pattern of compliance: about two-thirds of these districts appear to have changed their practices to conform to the Court's new prohibitions, while one-third acknowledge that they have not.[20] The regional variation is also evident, as shown in table 8.

TABLE 8

*Termination of Devotional Exercises*

| Region | Percentage of School Districts Stopping Devotionals | Number of Cases |
|--------|-----------------------------------------------------|-----------------|
| West | 62 | 21 |
| Midwest | 54 | 164 |
| East | 93 | 295 |
| South | 21 | 171 |

The close correspondence of these figures with those of the 1964 study of elementary teachers, cited above, should be noted. The West, where schoolhouse religion was rare to begin with, contributes too few cases for a reliable estimate, but practices appear nevertheless to have declined noticeably. The East, where homeroom devotionals were widespread, has complied almost totally. The South, whose devotional practices were also widespread, has largely resisted the Supreme Court mandate, complying in only one-fifth of the districts. And the Midwest, where religion in the schools was characteristic of a sizeable minority, has complied in about half the cases.

### Actions at the State Level
Why does compliance occur in some states, localities, or classrooms and not in others? At which institutions, officials, or processes does one look in order to explain why the consequences of this new national policy were so different in thousands of American classrooms? Many factors are at work, of course, but we must organize them in some conceptual scheme so that inquiry can proceed logically. Perhaps most significant in explaining the patterns of regional response just noted are actions taken by state-level authorities.

Broad currents of political tradition and practice help to shape the regional and state response patterns. Where a state has had a statutory requirement for some form of religious observance prior to the Court's ruling, it is more likely to respond in some official manner and thereby to create a uniform pattern of compliance or, in some cases, resistance. This is, generally speaking, what happened in the eastern and southern states respectively: action was taken by a state-level official or agency to promote or assure either compliance or noncompliance in the state as a whole. In the Midwest, this state-level action for the most part did not occur, as we shall now see.

An assessment of the significance of state-level policy is possible by comparing the compliance rates of states (as determined by our own resurvey of those districts with 1960 religious observances) with the actions taken (as of 1967) by relevant state-level agencies. Public records are available for four such agencies: the state legislature, the attorney general, the courts, and the state superintendent of education. In every case, any action taken since 1962 relevant to home-room devotional activity was noted as being in accord with the Supreme Court rulings or contradictory to them. For example, an attorney general may rule that *Schempp* now prohibits Bible reading in his state, or he may indicate that the law permits local districts to decide if they want to con-tinue the recitation of prayers in their schools. The legis-lature may change the statutes from requiring Bible reading to prohibiting it. The state superintendent may render an opinion that homeroom devotionals are now outlawed, or he may indicate that the Supreme Court's decisions have no bearing on the schools of his state. In many instances, of course, one or more of these agencies have taken no actions.

Table 9 classifies states by the number of their four agen-cies which took affirming and negating actions. Since few states were characterized by negating statements only, the final category contains two states with two "negatives" apiece, and four with one "negative" apiece. For each cate-gory, the compliance rate is the percentage of school districts (all engaged in homeroom devotions in 1960) which had stopped saying prayers and reading the Bible by 1967.

Clearly public statements by state officials are strongly related to the likelihood of compliance. If this relation is

TABLE 9

*Relation of Compliance Rates
to State-Level Policy Actions*

| State Agency Affirming–Negating Score | Number of States | Number of Districts | Compliance Rate |
|---|---|---|---|
| + 3 | 5 | 180 | 91% |
| + 2 | 7 | 141 | 89% |
| + 1 | 10 | 61 | 52% |
| 0 | 14 | 169 | 42% |
| −1 or −2 | 6 | 78 | 22% |

causal, we can, by noting the location of states with different scores, understand better the marked regional variation in compliance observed earlier. All of the six negating states are in the South, and eight of the twelve states with scores of + 2 or + 3 are eastern (two are midwestern, one is western, and one is border southern). Thus, strong public affirmation by state officials seems to promote a high rate of compliance, and public negation seems to inhibit it. In the majority of states, where state-level pronouncements are rare or nonexistent, the compliance is somewhat under 50 percent, suggesting the importance of factors below the statewide level in determining whether or not the schools comply. In the West, however, as we already noted, the practice of public school devotionals was rare before the *Schempp* decision and became rarer after it. It is in the region we designate as Midwest, therefore, where schoolhouse religion was reasonably common before 1962 and where it has declined noticeably (not so much as in the East but more than in the South), that we might best study the influence of minimal state-level direction or decision making. In six of these eleven midwestern states no public statement from legislature, attorney general, state superintendent, or court has been recorded; in three of the remaining five, there is evidence of only one such pronouncement. In the absence of state-level directives, then, we might infer that decisions to comply or not to comply were locally made.

## Summary

In this and the previous chapter we have reviewed evidence justifying our study's focus. With interest in the process by which national policy gets transposed (or fails to get transposed) into people's lives, we are about to analyze how a pair of Supreme Court decisions on schoolhouse religion were received by elites in one Midwestern state. In Chapter 2 we saw that, though *Engel* v. *Vitale* and *Schempp* were Court decisions relatively well known to the public, the Court's actions nonetheless remained the focus largely of leaders, officials, or elites. Changes induced by Supreme Court mandate, if carried out at all, are likely to be carried out by elites, not by the average citizen.

In Chapter 3 we noted the considerable regional variation in reception of the schoolhouse religion decisions and the related regional differences in the responses of state-level officials. We saw the Midwest to be an area where, on this issue, local factors had greater chances of operating. To observe the process of policy transposition where it is unencumbered by "decisive" intrusion of a single factor which by itself "settles" the matter, we turn therefore to the matter of schoolhouse religion in a midwestern state.

The chapters that follow tell, of course, an unrepresentative story; no single-issue investigation is likely to be "representative." Nevertheless following the analysis in Part 2 of Midway's responses to the school prayer decisions, we allow ourselves in Part 3 to speculate on the wider meaning our analysis might have in understanding national policies and local consequences.

# Part Two

# Responses in Midway

# 4 State Elites

## Letting Sleeping Dogs Lie

Mid–twentieth-century church-state relations in the state of Midway are as tangled and complex as they are remote in their origins. In this respect, of course, Midway resembles most states in the union. Its constitution, statutes, court decisions, and official practices contain extensive references to religion. Although it has never had either constitutional or legislative requirements for Bible reading or prayers in the schools, an 1865 statute declared that "The Bible shall not be excluded from the public schools of the state." Subsequent amendments and reenactments in 1907 and 1923 encouraged use of the Bible in "secular" (public) school courses. Statutory authorizations for released-time religious education and parochial-school busing have been on the books long enough to generate accretions of case law and several opinions of the state attorney general, particularly in periods subsequent to the major Supreme Court church-state decisions in 1947, 1948, and 1952.

This substantial body of legislation, official interpretation, and ad hoc rulings and precedents, however, authoritatively govern only a small proportion of the actual problems and practices in the area of church-school relations. Many varying local practices (baccalaureate services, religious observances, hymn-singing, prayers, pre-luncheon grace, Gideon Bible distribution, and countless teacher-innovated religious activities) owe their existence and legitimacy to custom and inertia rather than to official certification. Further, church-*school* relations are only a part of the larger problem area of the intersections of church and *state*. Although there is much overlap, and many analogies are possible, many salient questions of church-state relations do not involve the schools at all (e.g., taxability of church property; religious tests for office; Sunday closing laws; laws concerning abortion, divorce, or birth control information; coins; or legislative ceremonies.) Each of these other areas has produced a distinctive body of constitutional and legislative enactments, legal interpretations, and other rulings and practices. And, jointly and severally, the various facets of church-state and church-school relations have sparked continuing controversies among many groups and their shifting allies within the state.

The Supreme Court decisions of 1962 and 1963, therefore, did not introduce a new item onto Midway's political agenda. Indeed, there was a history of decades of precedents and battles in the arena of church-state relations. Combatants in this arena operate with long-established priorities and a reasonably clear view of both their own capabilities and their opponents'. Incompletely healed wounds, partially attained goals, and the prospect of a long-enduring relationship in the field are all factors contributing to a relatively realistic sense of the costs and benefits of various forms of action in response to the decisions.

Nor did the decisions at issue affect a broad segment of church-state or even of church-school relationships. The 1962 case banned the saying of state-composed prayer, and the 1963 cases outlawed the saying of the Lord's Prayer and the devotional reading of the Bible. All three cases rested on "establishment clause" grounds, to be sure, which suggested that all forms of school-sanctioned religious activities are unconstitutional, but even that interpretation left a wide range of other church-school questions untouched (indirect aid through textbook purchase and busing, to mention the most conflict-producing).

These Supreme Court decisions, therefore, involved only a fragment of a much more extensive set of issues, many of which were of long standing. Potential actors in this area not only had well-established priorities and multiple goals, but they also had an extended experience of dealing with each other and the prospect of its continuation long into the future. In this context, it becomes crucial for us to know the actual practices of local communities in regard to the matters covered by the Court's decisions: the status quo ante of local practice, if popularly supported, could in all probability be modified from above only by a major investment of time, energy, and other resources, to say nothing of the costs incurred in expenditure of good will or provocation of resentments. Actors at the state level, then, might understandably shape their strategies according to (1) their perceptions of the nature of the status quo, (2) the intensity of effort required to reshape it to that ordained by the Supreme Court, and (3) the importance of achieving such a goal in the first place.

### Local Practice in Midway at the Time of the Decisions

For reasons shortly to be specified, we doubt that a really accurate portrayal of schoolhouse religious practices could be obtained without sustained inspection of the actual classroom behavior of a very large sample of teachers in the state of Midway. A survey conducted under the auspices of the Midway School Boards Association in early 1964, however, provides a beginning. When interpreted in the light of our interviewing experience, the results may approximate a characterization of sufficient accuracy for our purposes. The survey was conducted by the state university's school of education and elicited an 86 percent response from Midway's more than 250 school district superintendents; it was introduced by a covering letter from the executive secretary of the School Board Association, and confidentiality and anonymity were assured to respondents. A total of twenty-two yes-no or check-off questions sought to measure the extent of various forms of religious activity in Midway schools.

Perhaps the most significant finding of this survey appeared in response to its final question: "Has your school district made any change of policy regarding religion and the public schools as a result of either or both of the recent Supreme

Court decisions relative to prayer and Bible reading?" Ninety-five percent of responding superintendents declared that there had been no change in policy. Whatever was being done before 1962 or 1963, in other words, was apparently still being done in 1964. But a clarifying note must be entered at this point: school board policy, in the sense of official rules or formalized instructions to teachers, is to be sharply distinguished from actual teacher practice, itself varyingly encouraged by informal means within the school system.[1] Very few school boards had official policies requiring or authorizing the reading of the Bible or the saying of prayers before 1962. If the responding superintendent answered strictly in terms of official policy, a "no change" answer could reflect the fact that no change in official policy was necessarily mandated by the Court's decisions. Thus, the 95 percent negative response rate could mean that school boards had failed to initiate a new official policy to the effect that prayers could *not* be said. In the light of a tradition of not having official policy of any kind on this subject, such failure might be understandable.

But a substantial body of other evidence suggests that the real implication of this answer is that there was no change from previous actual teacher practice of saying prayers and reading the Bible. For one thing, comments accompanying responses to this question emphasized that teachers continued as they had been doing, or that the "problem" would not be raised unless "undue pressure" were exerted. Other comments on the general subject of the relation between religion and the schools indicated a strong feeling that the connection was a healthy one and should continue until "the problem is agitated." A typical response reads in full:

The way I interpret this is that school boards, state, etc., cannot prescribe a certain religious prayer. I feel that the teacher,

1. In asking whether particular forms of religious activities were conducted, the survey had earlier distinguished school board negative policy, school board affirmative policy, school board permissive or authorizing policy, and teacher practice in the absence of any board policy. Our interviewing within school districts, however, made it clear that the distinction is a formalistic and illusory one: in some cases where the board had no formal written policy, superintendents regularly appeared in the schools and themselves conducted religious activities. The ways in which boards, superintendents, and principals can make known their preference for or unconcern about religious activities are far too numerous (and subtle) for accurate representation by survey questions.

on her own volition, may use religious readings, prayer, etc., as long as it is not offensive to a child. In that event, I think the child can be excluded for that portion which is offensive to him. We plan to continue until *forced* to stop. (Italics in original)

In this and many other cases, comments also indicated that superintendents viewed the question as one of the freedom to worship. In other words, they transposed the grounds of the decisions. What began as an establishment clause prohibition (the state may not sponsor the saying of prayers or the reading of the Bible because that would be establishing religion) became an issue of religious freedom (the state may not prevent those who wish to say prayers from doing so). We shall explore this cognitive transposition more fully in a later chapter.

The survey itself provides considerable evidence that actual practice within the schools included widespread Bible reading and saying of prayers. In answer to a query as to whether the Bible was read at the opening of school each day, 8 percent of respondents said that this was permitted by school board policy and 28 percent said that there was no board policy but that it was practiced in one or more schools by one or more teachers. Sixty-three percent answered that *"to my knowledge"* it was not practiced. To another query, 9 percent reported that board policy permitted some prayer recitation led by a pupil or teacher, and 52 percent acknowledged that this was the practice in the absence of board policy. These data do not indicate that prayers were said by a total of 61 percent of all pupils or teachers but rather that such proportions of school superintendents were aware and willing to report that board policy authorized it or that one or more teachers did so in one or more of their schools. At the very least, here is concrete evidence of substantial violation of the Supreme Court's rulings.

But, for several reasons, we believe that these data support the judgment that such proscribed exercises were more systematic and widespread in actual practice, and were not just scattered occurrences attributable to the idiosyncrasies of a few teachers. Our interviewing convinces us (again, for reasons to be more fully explored in a later chapter) that Midway superintendents have developed a specialized perception in this subject area, particularly noticeable in their answers to questionnaire-type inquiries, which leads them to respond in terms of their boards' official policies rather than actual teacher practice. Despite questionnaire responses indicating full compliance with the Court's rulings, for example, where-ever we examined actual practice we found prayers or Bible reading or other religious observances clearly proscribed by the Court.[2] We also found a kind of professional ignorance, or unwillingness to know what was going on, which leads us to view as understatement all assertions that could take advantage of this survey's escape clause that "to my knowledge" the various religious exercises were not practiced. Perhaps this effect is understandable where officials are being asked in effect to acknowledge that persons under their jurisdiction are not observing the law of the land. In any event, we are inclined to attribute even wider religious activity to the schools of Midway than the survey responses themselves would indicate.

Further evidence of the suffusion of the schools with religious activities and observances emerges from other responses in the survey. In 80 percent of the school districts, Gideon Bibles are distributed to children, usually by a Gideon representative handing them to children in their classrooms. Baccalaureate services are held by 95 percent of the school districts, on school property in 76 percent and with compulsory attendance in 26 percent. Singing of religious hymns was acknowledged by 52 percent, and of Christmas carols by all; ministers, rabbis, and priests took part in school assembly programs in 67 percent of the school districts responding. No question was asked about that activity which our interviewing found to be most common, the saying of grace before lunch in the elementary schools, although many respondents volunteered that they did so. Although only 9 percent of the superintendents acknowledged that released time for religious education on school property (held unconstitutional by the Court as far back as 1948) still took place in their schools, a comment by one such respondent sums up the realities of the social and institutional support for religious practices in the schools:

> In two of our schools, two ladies teach Bible lessons thirty minutes once every two weeks to children at the fourth, fifth, and sixth grade level. Only those pupils who want to take

2. See the Appendix for a discussion of the sequence of research strategies we employed. The "questionnaire responses" referred to are explained there.

these classes participate in them. This has been in effect in the schools for several years. I have talked to many parents in the school district, and they do not want me or the school board to interfere with this instruction. It has not been officially approved or disapproved by the board.

What could be more innocuous than the "two ladies" and Bible classes? But the structural support for teachers who choose to engage in religious activities within the schools would probably be even stronger than the support given by this superintendent to outsiders engaged in the nearly extinct (and illegal) practice of released time on school property.

It seems likely, although we cannot present reliable evidence, that prayers and Bible reading were in effect as a routine matter in at least half of the elementary school classrooms throughout Midway at the time of the Supreme Court's decisions in 1962 and 1963. The pattern of religious activity in the schools was far from uniform; it was ad hoc and widely variant from district to district, depending on a host of extraneous factors. But it seems clear that it was widespread—and also clear that it was inconsistent with the law of the land.

### State Officials' Reactions to the Decisions

What cues did visible and relevant (in the sense of having official responsibility for enforcement) state-level elites provide for local guidance with regard to the Supreme Court's decisions? In the light of the foregoing description of the nature of actual local practice, perhaps we should also ask, To what extent were these cues given because of, or at least with the knowledge of, contemporary practice in the schools? A review of the actions of state-level agents reveals almost universal rejection of the Court's decisions and their possible implications. State officials themselves can be differentiated by the extent to which they had knowledge of actual practice, but nearly all of the relevant state-level officials and others perceived clearly the substance of the mandate of the Supreme Court. Very few failed to understand the decisions, although some were inclined to overstate potential implications in the course of flights of denunciatory rhetoric. We shall review the reactions of state officials in order of ascending likelihood of their knowledge of practices within the state.

Initial reaction to *Engel* v. *Vitale* was sharp and negative. Representatives of the three major faiths of Midway provided the umbrella under which officials could proceed to denounce both the decisions and the Court. The Episcopalian bishop declared, "The Supreme Court and such groups as the Civil Liberties Union ought soon to realize that religious groups have rights also which are being denied them by such decisions." The Methodist bishop concurred: "The decision lends unfortunate support to the idea that the majority has no rights. That in moral and spiritual matters, whatever a minority objects to must be stopped." And the chancellor of the Catholic archdiocese added, "The need for prayer is already proven, and these truths are not going to be found in court decisions or scientific manuals."

The moderate tone of these religious leaders contrasted sharply with the language of those key officials who might be expected to carry responsibility for shaping public reaction to the decisions and who certainly hold official responsibility for the enforcement of such decisions. The chief justice of the Midway State Supreme Court, for example, charged the United States Supreme Court with "playing recklessly with the Constitution of this country." He issued a statement ("speaking as an individual attorney") saying that citizens are "fully justified in criticizing the decision," which "any person of average intelligence can see is a distorted and unwarranted extension of a constitutional provision to matters not included therein." The chief justice went on to a more general critique of the Supreme Court:

Many good lawyers shake their heads in humiliation at the reflection which the United States Supreme Court creates upon the bench and bar as a whole in this country. To those who say we should respect the high court, my answer is that it has certainly created its own contempt and lack of respect by its disregard of the Constitution. Not all lawyers are overawed or spellbound by the decisions of that court, but rather are embarrassed with the lack of legal knowledge revealed in them.

The attorney general of Midway offered his analysis a few days later, though still only a week after the 1962 decision was announced. He had been one of twenty-two attorneys general to join New York on the brief in defense of the state's "Regents Prayer." Confessing "confusion" over the Supreme Court's ruling, he asked an interviewer rhetorically, "We believe in the philosophy of separation of church and state, but how far can this go?" Acknowledging that he had heard "periodic complaints" about religious observances in schools, "mostly from the Midway Civil Liberties Union and the Anti-

Defamation League," the attorney general offered his own philosophy as the only guidance available: "It doesn't shock my conscience that we have religious pageants and sing Christmas carols in the schools." Not to be outdone, even though he was less intimately involved in enforcement responsibilities, the United States district attorney for the state of Midway ("speaking only as a Catholic layman") subsequently declared that he did not believe in the complete separation of church and state, chiefly because the founders of the Constitution did not intend such.

Thus, by the time of the 1963 decisions, all three of the key figures in potential enforcement in Midway were on record publicly against the Court's policies. There was no change in their positions after the *Schempp* and *Murray* cases. Indeed, if anything, they were joined by others of nearly equal stature. Another judge of the Midway Supreme Court, for example, writing a letter to the editor of a daily newspaper, urged support of constitutional amendments to allow prayer in the schools. Declaring that, "it was no more logical to prohibit the children of New York from repeating this reverent but simple prayer because it contained the seeds of a state church than it would be to argue that no man be permitted to start a business in his garage because of the possibility that he might monopolize the industry," the judge went on to review the history of religious exercises in the United States. His argument is typical of many public pronouncements by Midway officialdom in this period:

In our schools, prayer and the reading of the Bible were an approved, if not a prescribed practice from the founding of our country. Thanksgiving, Christmas, and Easter exercises, all religious activities, were the most significant events in the school calendar. In the tradition of these religious declarations and practices, America has been blessed above all other nations. America has thus verified the Biblical exultation that "Blessed is the nation whose God is the Lord."
But now we are told by our courts and a few clergymen that these practices of 200 years are all wrong and can no longer be tolerated. We are told that the proper place for the teaching and practice of religion is in the home and in the church, and not in the public schools. But can we expect greater respect for religion, greater morality, fewer dropouts from schools, or less delinquency and crime, by removing all religious teaching and practices from our schools? The evidence is otherwise.
Religion is neither taught nor practiced in most of the homes of America. Is the church equal to the need? A large percentage

of our people are not affiliated with any church, and many who are church affiliates are no more than that. Furthermore, most children who attend church are under its influence no more than one hour a week. The church and the home need all the support and assistance possible in developing today's child "in the way he should go." The Bible commands: "In all thy ways acknowledge Him." To me this includes not only the home and the church, but also the schools.

These reactions, of course, may be exclusively directed at the propriety of the Supreme Court's decisions, and not intended to be, nor in fact indicative of, what these key officials would do in the event of a court challenge to Bible reading or saying prayers in the Midway schools. And there is no evidence, moreover, that any of these significant figures knew the extent to which prayers and other religious observances were a fact of life in Midway schools; nor does it necessarily appear that they were consciously giving assurances to local elites that such activities could continue. But the effect of their pronouncements can hardly have been lost upon others in the state.

Where these officials may be seen as expressing their personal preferences (albeit from an official position of significance within the state) in the absence of knowledge about actual practices, a different characterization must be made of the actions and statements of the Midway state superintendent of public instruction—the state's leading educational official. The incumbent was a man of extensive experience ("I've been in the school business 45 years . . .") who could hardly have been unaware of established practices. He was also the man to whom professionally oriented school district superintendents were most likely to look for guidance about the changes, if any, which would be required as a result of these decisions. Queried by a newspaper the day after *Engel* v. *Vitale* was announced, the superintendent said, "I am very sorry to see a decision like that made. . . . There is nothing our office can do as far as sending out instructions to the schools. I was sort of surprised. . . . It's pretty hard to isolate the human race from a Supreme Being."

Four days later, the leading newspaper in the state devoted a feature column to the possible implications of the Supreme Court's decision. The superintendent of the school system in the state capital, also Midway's largest city and the site of the state superintendent of instruction's offices, declared that

there would be no change in city practices. At that time the
city's school board had a policy which stated:

The morning exercises of each school may include the reading
or reciting of the Scriptures or other appropriate matter, and
that exercise may be followed by the repetition of the Lord's
Prayer and by appropriate singing. Teachers shall guard
against introducing subjects of a sectarian or partisan religious
character [sic].

A school official was quoted as saying that "a sizeable number" of teachers regularly had such religious exercises in
class. In the same feature story, the state superintendent of
public instruction was quoted as acknowledging, "Quite a
few schools in Midway have Scripture readings and devotions," but that complaints had arisen only in the past ten
years. "And then the complaints were mild— and few." He
again assured his interviewer that there would be no need to
issue an administrative order as a result of the high court's
decision. Nor did he modify his laissez faire position with the
passage of time. In 1963, just before the next pair of decisions, he assured a public audience that "We can have a separation of church and state, yet have religion in the schools,
because the teachers' attitudes transmit it to students."

The state superintendent's frank acknowledgement that the
schools practiced various forms of religious observances
marks him as the only major Midway official who can authoritatively be said to have known of the extent of local practice. But several daily newspapers throughout the state
carried repeated articles quoting local school superintendents
as vowing to continue teacher-initiated religious practices, so
that a reasonably attentive official (or even a layman) might
have been alerted to the realities of the Midway schools. These
articles appeared at intervals after both *Engel* v. *Vitale* and
after the 1963 decisions. A typical feature story of this kind,
shortly after the *Engel* announcement, read as follows:

No change in the practice of prayer in public schools in
—— and —— is expected by superintendents of the three
country school districts as a result of the recent U.S. Supreme
Court ruling.
    The high court's decision barred as unconstitutional a law
in the state of New York prescribing a particular form of
prayer to be delivered by school children.
    Supt. —— of the —— Metropolitan School District said he
believes Midway is not caught up in the controversy.

"If there were such a law in Midway, stating that children had to pray or had to read the Bible, then the ruling clearly would affect us.

"I don't believe the court ruling states that we can't use God in our teaching. . . . We don't have any formal policy, and therefore have no conflicts."

——, who formerly was a principal in —— County schools, added that he could foresee no change in the practice of prayer in the classrooms here.

"We will continue to have ministers in as speakers, we are going to pray, hold baccalaureate services and things like that. . . . If a second grade teacher wants to have her children offer grace before lunch, that is perfectly all right as far as I'm concerned."

——, superintendent of the four unconsolidated township schools in southern —— County, and ——, superintendent of the —— Schools, a consolidation of four northern townships, agreed that the ruling would have no immediate effect here.

"I would have to say that I disagree with the Supreme Court decision," Supt. —— stated, "although I feel there has to be a careful balance of how much religion is taught."

—— said he supported interpretations of the Constitution which barred sectarian teaching of religion in public schools. But he added that as he read the "Regent's Prayer" which was the subject of the Supreme Court ruling, it was a "non-denomination and nonsectarian prayer."

"We probably have no standard policy of prayer in —— County—I must say 'probably' because I do not know for sure," he stated. "Formal observances of prayer in most of the schools might be limited to grace before noon meals.

"Generally, the teaching of prayers has been left to the in-dividual teacher. I can't imagine running into a conflict in this practice and I don't expect any change."

Supt. —— said he believed all teachers have observed a practice of avoiding sectarian teaching. Generally, the schools have concentrated in the implanting of Christian principles in students, he said.

"Our policy in this regard may not be changed, but we could be stymied a little bit (by the court ruling)."

The same kind of story reported similar facts and reactions in several daily papers in the months following the *Schempp* and *Murray* decisions. Many superintendents reported that their schools' religious activities were "purely voluntary" and "left to the discretion of the classroom teacher," so that the Court's decisions were "inapplicable." Several stressed par-ents' support for such activities, one declaring that "law suits are instigated by cranks who like the publicity." Without exception, the school superintendents publicly quoted made assertions that Bible reading and prayers would continue "as in the past" until someone raised an objection and made it stick.

The reporting of such position-taking by school superintendents was frequent and repeated. It seems clear that responsible officials, including all whose reactions have been surveyed so far, *could* have known the nature of local practice, and perhaps *should* have known of it, merely by being attentive readers of any one of several daily newspapers. At some point on the continuum of available knowledge, ignorance begins to appear more deliberate than coincidental. Under such circumstances, it may be unfair to single out the state superintendent of public instruction's knowledgeable and yet laissez faire position for special comment.

Some officials, such as the justices of the Midway Supreme Court or the United States district attorney, had no power or responsibility to initiate efforts to secure compliance in this area. In the absence of litigation brought by private parties, their roles were limited to public cue-giving. But both the attorney general and the state superintendent of public instruction were heads of state agencies which could have initiated action of various kinds to move the Midway schools closer to the Supreme Court's policies, if not in total conformity with them. Some modest or token instruction to local districts, or a perfunctory acknowledgement of the Court's decision, might have constituted a rational strategy for creating the appearance of compliance or providing local districts with insulation against local pressures to comply more fully. But neither state agency acted in any way: no opinion, instruction, circular letter, or memorandum on the subject had emerged from either agency in six years subsequent to the *Engel* decision. Interviews within each department provided some insight into the reasons for such quiescence.

Although the Office of the Attorney General was not large during this period (averaging between fifteen and twenty staff members), there was a deputy attorney general for educational affairs, reporting in turn to a senior deputy attorney general and thence to the elected attorney general. Two themes were expressed by the deputies in interviews: the first was that "of course" compliance was complete in Midway because the Supreme Court's rulings were clear; and the second (apparently a fall-back position) was that the issue was not yet a matter of political controversy, and therefore it would be better to "let sleeping dogs lie." The two men who held the position of deputy for educational affairs during the six years after *Engel* both professed amazement that there were indications of noncompliance within the state, as well as resentment at the fact that an interviewer would raise the question. Both asserted confidently that it was not the function of the state attorney general's office to act in this field; there were "enough hot potatoes" without raising such issues. On one such issue, that of school busing, however, an official opinion was sought by legislators, and the attorney general used the opportunity to brusquely dismiss the possibility that one could seriously question the constitutionality of parochial-school bus laws. But, no opinion having been sought through official channels in regard to school religious activities, none was rendered. Indeed, it appeared that one of the incumbents was not knowledgeable on this subject at all: despite detailed assistance he was unable to distinguish *Engel* from *Schempp* and *Murray*. This was another in a series of cognitive failures typical of many actors in this policy area. Several officials at various levels had accomplished the same complete "blanking-out" of the 1963 cases, although they were lucid and precise on *Engel* and frequently also on several lower court cases from other states.

The deputy attorney general with oversight responsibility for educational affairs viewed his office similarly as a passive agency for opinion-rendering *when requested*. He confirmed that not even informal guidance had been sought or provided, that the Supreme Court's rulings were beyond the legal (not just the practical) capacity of the state Attorney General's Office to enforce. Although he personally declared his support for the Court's decisions (thereby becoming the first state officer to do so, even in a private interview), it was clear that he saw the legal apparatus of the state as powerless in this area. When pressed on the problem of relating federal laws and court decisions to the practices at the local level, he threw up his hands and cried, *"Federal laws? Nobody* understands *federal laws!"*

The same general laissez faire policy, limited perceptions of power, and mild opposition to the Court's rulings prevailed in the Office of the State Superintendent of Public Instruction. The top three officials are known as the "political" men, although only the superintendent is actually elected. As

State Elites **53**

Democrats surrounded by Republican officeholders on the state level, the superintendent and his chief deputies are anxious to avoid controversy. But so are the lower echelons of career personnel in the office, and none of them pressed for any form of confrontation despite the contrast between Supreme Court rulings and local practice. The key officials for this subject area are a curriculum director and the applicable assistant state superintendent. Although both privately asserted their agreement as professional educators with the Court's decisions, both felt it better to "let sleeping dogs lie" (independently volunteered). Official knowledge of actual local practice was avoided by the simple expedient of not seeking any form of statistics on such matters, but both men were aware of the local practices and confident that district superintendents felt quite safe in continuing them. Neither saw it as any part of his role in such circumstances to make an issue out of the matter, even within the confines of the department. Both could recall references by their superiors to President Jackson's oft-quoted remark that "John Marsall has made his decision; now let him enforce it," and to Stalin's query about the number of divisions possessed by the Pope. They thought compliance probable only in three communities which held universities, with their heterogeneous and active faculties, and in the state's largest city after a long series of public controversies. Despite the pessimism, the issue was apparently not important enough to raise to the level of principle within their department.

The pattern of response by state officials is therefore one of almost universal and public rejection, accompanied by deliberate inaction on the part of those with authority to initiate enforcement of various kinds. Except for one or two cases, men at this level correctly perceived the nature of the Court's rulings; they were not in doubt that first a state-composed prayer and then the recitation of the Lord's Prayer and the Bible were held unconstitutional. At least the top hierarchy of the State Office of Public Instruction, and quite possibly others as well, were aware that the Midway practice was not only to avoid policy statements by local school boards but also to engage routinely and widely in such activities on a publicly acknowledged "teacher-discretion" basis. In all probability, most members of the attentive public also understood the nature of local practice, and perhaps their public officials took this into account in designing their own responses. But public officials do not act solely with regard to either their own or perceived public preference, and we must therefore survey the types of pressure brought to bear on them by various major organizations and groups.

**Interest-Group Reactions to the Decisions**
We found a total of seven groups whose interests and activities touched upon the issue of religious observances in the Midway public schools. Two of these are semiofficial associations of persons professionally engaged in the administration of the schools: the Midway School Board Association and the Midway Teachers Association. Four others are religious or special-interest groups with unique concern for civil liberties and particularly for freedom of religion issues: the Midway Civil Liberties Union, the Midway Council of Churchs, the Anti-Defamation League of B'nai B'rith, and the National Conference of Christians and Jews. Each of these maintains in the state capital an office affiliated with the respective national organization, and each has a full-time staff performing clearing-house and informational functions for local units within the state. Finally, the state PTA also maintains a headquarters in the state capital and displays a sporadic concern for the questions at issue. We shall briefly review their reactions in order.

The Midway School Board Association is a membership organization of nearly all of the 250 school boards in the state. It is housed in the School of Education at the state university, where its executive secretary holds a professorial position with teaching responsibilities in the area of school law. Continuing leadership is also provided by an executive committee elected from the regions of the state. The principal activities of the association include leadership training for new school board members, an annual convention, some research and service efforts for the membership, fairly frequent legislative lobbying, and publication of the *Midway School Board Association Journal*. In practice, most of the three-man staff's energy is devoted to legislative lobbying, participation as amicus curiae and other legal services for inquiring school boards, and the collection of various statistics on school operations in Midway.

Very little formal action was taken by the association in regard to schoolhouse religious activities. Immediately after the *Schempp* and *Murray* cases, a six-page analysis of the holding and its implications was sent out to members as one in a series of occasional School Board Bulletins. The document is a fairly straightforward and accurate account of the issues and opinions in the two cases, clearly reporting the establishment-clause grounds on which they rested. In the final section entitled "Implications of the Decision," however, the bulletin points out that the holdings did not necessarily mandate change in Midway:

> Even though the decision applies only to specific situations in Pennsylvania and Maryland, it seems clear that no state or agent of the state (such as a local school board) may constitutionally *require* the reading of any version of the Holy Bible or the use of any particular prayer in the public schools. The situation here, however, is much the same as in the area of segregation; segregation continues in many American school districts today in spite of the 1954 desegregation decision of the United States Supreme Court. Until a plaintiff actually brings a suit in mandamus, applying to a specific violation, an unconstitutional practice may continue for years.

The language is not unambiguous, but in the context of Midway practices the message communicated seems to be one of reassurance that "teacher-discretion" still enjoyed a long life expectancy.

The association did sponsor the survey of Midway school district practices referred to earlier in this chapter. The results were tabulated without much analysis and with no comment, and the report was distributed to the membership as one of a series of occasional Research Bulletins. The only other contact with religious questions which would have been visible to the membership through the association was an article by a Methodist bishop in a 1968 issue of the monthly *Journal,* in which the author advocated a number of religious educational programs not proscribed by the Court. Noting that the Court had left open the use of the Bible as a source for literary or historical instruction, the  bishop specifically endorsed a program, locally known, of prepared course materials and teacher-training outlines for such Bible study. Reporting that these materials were in use in "more than a dozen Midway communities," the bishop asserted that this is an effective way to communicate knowledge about the contents of the Bible without imposing sectarian or devotional demands upon students. Analysis of the one-man lobbyist's prepared materials indicates that, at least as written, they conform to the Court's allowance for use of the Bible as literature.

Two men held the post of executive secretary of the School Board Association during the six years subsequent to the *Engel* case. The office changed hands in 1967, as a result of the death of the first incumbent, but the well-established style of operation apparently remained constant. Both men were former school superintendents who saw their roles as administrators of the decisions taken by the association's executive committee; neither has had a private stake in shaping the programs or actions of the association itself, and neither appears to have made any such effort. The general ethos of the organization, therefore, was less that of the professional educators' thrust toward organizational efficiency and achievement than the board members' need for political support, funds, and services.

The second incumbent, Dr. T., divides his nonteaching time between keeping abreast of legislative developments and lawsuits involving Midway school systems and editing the *Journal*. This set of interests, together with the legal nature of his teaching duties, led him to become one of the most informed persons in the entire state of Midway regarding the holdings of the Supreme Court.

He understood the Court's position in absolutist terms, that is, all forms of religious observances, whether teacher-initiated or not, were forbidden. Further, he declared his firm personal support for such a position, both on grounds of the desirability of detaching the public schools from all involvement with religion, and because of the respect in which he held the Court as an institution. Nevertheless, he denied all knowledge of what actual practice was in the various school districts of the state, declaring with apparent sincerity that he "didn't know" what the practices were in the school district where he had been superintendent until he moved to his present position not a year earlier. He had not studied, and indeed could barely recall, the survey distributed by the association less than four years previously.

The posture of the association—as essentially a service-providing agency—would have foreclosed initiation of any advice to members on such a matter in any event. Dr. T. did not see his own views as relevant, therefore, nor could he recall any consideration of this issue by the executive committee. Many other questions created controversy at conven-

tions, some in the religious field, such as released time and
school busing, but apparently schoolhouse religious activities
had such little importance that the association never found
itself confronted with choices on this subject. This may be
another way of saying that the degree of consensus on maintaining "teacher-discretion" (and thereby having a variety of
religious observances with a minimum of public controversy)
is so great that the matter is not even on members' minds.

The Midway State Teachers Association, in some respects
the political antagonist of the School Board Association,
nevertheless shares many of the same reasons for not getting
involved with schoolhouse religion questions. The organization itself is much more of a personal vehicle, having been
started in the late 1930s by Mr. D., a politically astute, former
teacher who still served as executive secretary in 1968. From
his position as chief executive officer and editor of the primary communication vehicle (*The Midway Teacher,* a
monthly journal which he founded at the same time he
formed the association), Mr. D. has developed substantial
political influence over the entire spectrum of educational
issues and offices in the state of Midway. Officials in the
Attorney General's Office and in the Office of the State
Superintendent of Public Instruction report that no major
actions are taken, nor nominations for educational offices
made, without consulting Mr. D. Within Mr. D.'s own staff,
the reasons seem obvious: *The Midway Teacher* reaches
about 100,000 teacher-voters, and no politician is anxious
to appear in a bad light before such an audience.

But the exercise of such influence on behalf of that large a
constituency also imposes some constraints. In order to maintain constituency support, the journal must be of service to individuals, and it must not be provocative of controversy which
would divide the membership. In order to focus political
influence on the subjects which matter most, the organization
must not take on unnecessary causes or create undesirable
tensions. The chief goals of the Teachers Association center
on salary, tenure, and working conditions, and there was no
inclination anywhere to take up the schoolhouse religion
questions. The staff attorney with nominal responsibility for
such an area confined himself (even privately) to the narrow-
est possible interpretations of the Court's rulings, with the
expressed purpose of interfering minimally with the teachers'
preferences and activities.

In these circumstances, it is not surprising to find that the sole involvement of the association with the prayer and Bible reading issues consisted of three neutral "legal interpretation" articles in *The Midway Teacher,* written by a professor of education law at a major Midway university. Two articles in the fall of 1963 presented a comprehensive analysis of the Court's holdings, and a year later another article restated the various uses of the Bible and prayers that were not held unconstitutional. The first two articles, predictably, were technical and exhaustive in presenting the opinions of the justices. The third was written in part as a result of the author's experience with his students, most of whom were teachers in the Midway schools; he found that interpretations varied widely and that confusion over the two decisions was widespread. Again neutral, the final article describes how some schools are doing too much in the way of compliance, and some not enough. Pointing out that schools may still constitutionally teach about religion, he endorsed many of the same activities (identifying the same local source of materials) referred to by the Methodist bishop in the *School Board Association Journal.* "It is not necessary, nor is it wise, to completely remove religion from the public schools," he wrote. "Even though the Supreme Court has banned prayers imposed by the state, it has definitely not banned all . . . prayer from our schools." Arguing from freedom of religion premises, he concludes that children cannot be prevented from saying prayers before meals nor from having the opportunity for periods of silent meditation.

Both of these organizations have well-established and strongly supported memberships with vested interests in the manner in which the schools are run. Both include a substantial emphasis on professional standards and efficiently operated schools. But neither saw fit to raise schoolhouse religion to the level of an issue. In contrast, the four civil libertarian groups paid careful attention to the merits of the issue and took it upon themselves to act in some fashion to further the Court's rulings. But they were not well established, they seriously lacked legitimacy and influence, and their memberships were pitifully small and isolated. Their characteristic self-image was one of great vulnerability, so much so that they were likely to spend most of their energies denying that their national headquarters had anything to do with bringing the original cases before the Supreme Court.

The Midway Civil Liberties Union, like many such groups, relies upon the devoted efforts of a handful of staff and long-term members, supplemented from time to time, as issues arise, by a thin scattering of local support among attorneys and intellectuals throughout the state. During the post-decision period here involved, only five active local affiliates existed in the entire state of Midway. The capital city office was operated by an executive secretary and three staff assistants; the president, a capital city dentist, was on hand for release of public statements when necessary.

The Civil Liberties Union body with principal responsibility for schoolhouse religion issues is its Church-State Committee, which for this entire period was chaired by an active and knowledgeable CLU founder, Dr. S., who is also the executive secretary of the Midway Council of Churches. In his joint capacity, Dr. S. was a major source of what impetus there was toward compliance with the Court's rulings. He understood and thoroughly endorsed the Court's holdings and their implications. But despite his sincerity and attention to this question, he too was unwilling to force it into public controversy, and he too (apparently) deflected knowledge of the extent of "teacher-discretion" in the schools.

To begin with, the Midway Civil Liberties Union was suspect and defensive. In 1968 it was still unable to gain the use of a major arena in the state's capital city without court action—because of the taint of "subversion" associated with it. Much of its efforts was directed at remaining afloat, and no major campaign could be initiated regarding prayer in the schools without again seriously endangering its public image. Under these circumstances, its choice of private channels for expressing its views is understandable. Dr. S. initiated a conference with the state superintendent of public instruction, at which he and the executive secretaries of the other civil liberties groups jointly requested the superintendent to issue an instruction to school boards concerning the elimination of prayers in the schools. The superintendent of course refused to do so, pleading noninterference with the responsibilities and prerogatives of local authorities. Dr. S. and his colleagues had to content themselves with providing materials

for use by the superintendent when questions were referred
to his office—an expedient surely better calculated to save
face for them than to achieve results from the superintendent.

In his 1964 report to the membership on behalf of the
Church-State Committee, Dr. S. noted this apparently un-
satisfactory compromise, but he offered no program for
further action. Several other issues also occupied the committee during this period of relative prominence of the Court's
religion decisions—issues like the repeal of state laws concerning interracial marriage and ministerial counseling thereof,
change in the definitions of the religious basis for claiming
conscientious objector status, the Becker Amendment (which
would alter the Constitution to allow schoolhouse religion),
and school busing. This existence of other and perhaps more
serious intrusions upon church-state separation or religious
freedom was an important reason for the Civil Liberties
Union's reluctance to force the issue over prayer and Bible
reading. In its 1965 report to the membership, for example,
the committee touched upon one school system's publicly
asserted belief-in-God requirement for employment, a controversy over distribution of Gideon Bibles, issues in public
aid to higher education, Operation Head Start, and the administration of the Elementary and Secondary Education Act
of 1965. Action in regard to the school-prayer question, therefore, was limited to a public statement by the president of
the Midway chapter opposing the Becker Amendment and
urging the people of Midway to support the Court's decisions.

In his other capacity as executive secretary of the Midway
Council of Churches, Dr. S. had on the surface a greater
freedom of choice and more resources to develop influence—
but the result was much the same. The Council of Churches
is affiliated with the National Council of Churches, the largest
and most influential organization of Protestant churches in
the United States. Many local churches and church leaders
are members. As editor of the *Midway Church Councilor,*
Dr. S. had an opportunity to shape opinion. But the Midway
Council of Churches also suffered from local suspicion, and
a long history of bitter battles resulting from the liberal positions taken by its leaders in unpopular causes led it to
proceed very cautiously in controversial matters. In particular,
a long conflict over released-time issues had left barely healed
wounds in precisely this area. Member churches would probably have resisted any attempt on Dr. S.'s part to put the

Council on record as supporting the Court decisions; if anything of this kind had come up, the vote probably would have gone against the Court. More subtle efforts to build support for the Court would probably have met similar reactions. As a consequence, only one modest article appeared in the *Councilor* in the six years after *Engel,* and that was in March 1966, when a list of religious-type activities not proscribed by the Court was published on a back page.

Dr. S. did not view his situation as one of defeat or frustration. He was able to express his personal views in several ways, and his position as executive secretary lent special weight to his arguments. Much of his time in the years immediately after *Engel* was spent in answering specific queries about the implications of the decisions and in speaking around the state. In conjunction with representatives of the Anti-Defamation League and the National Conference of Christians and Jews, for example, he developed a program which sought to prepare editors and reporters for the 1963 decisions. Conferences were held at key locations in the state at which Dr. S. (apparently because of his Protestant credentials) was the featured speaker. He acknowledged in an interview that a widespread taint of "communism" surrounding the Council of Churches was a handicap, but he nevertheless felt that on the merits of the schoolhouse religion issue he was able to gain a fair hearing from the relatively sophisticated audiences which his program drew.

Perhaps naturally, Dr. S. viewed his achievements in a more optimistic light than would a more dispassionate observer. By 1968 his recollection was that the state superintendent had in fact issued the instruction to school boards which he and his colleagues had sought. He attributed more success to the predecision conferences of 1963 than seems warranted by subsequent reactions. And he also insisted that he had no knowledge of local practices of "teacher-discretion" prayers and other religious activities in the schools, expressing the characteristic resentment at the implication of the question.

The local units of the Anti-Defamation League and the National Conference of Christians and Jews had a different set of constraints and resources to deal with in their efforts to promote church-state separation. For one thing, in a thoroughly Protestant state, they are chiefly Jewish in staff, origins, and support. Perhaps for this reason they have not ventured into public controversy. They are scarcely visible, let alone tainted with a subversive image—though they could undoubtedly have acquired one quickly. Because their membership is much smaller than even the other two civil libertarian groups, they can have no hope of developing vote-based influence, and indeed their operating techniques have never contemplated such an approach. If anything, their small membership is an advantage because it precludes internal constraints and prevents divisions from arising. Moreover, financial support, research services, and policy guidance are frequently available from their national headquarters.

The Anti-Defamation League and the National Council of Christians and Jews worked very closely together, and in conjunction with Dr. S.'s organizations, to advance the cause of separation of church and state in Midway. National headquarters of ADL distributed collections of statements supporting the Court rulings for use by local speakers, as well as copies of surveys made of the extent of compliance around the country. The informational exchange conducted within the internal channels of the ADL is impressive in both quantity and quality. NCCJ's ideas for the predecision conferences to prepare editors and reporters for understanding and accurately interpreting the 1963 decisions thus fits naturally with the primary interest and emphasis of ADL. Three formal conferences on this theme were held in the spring of 1963, to the satisfaction of all the sponsors. NCCJ also joined with local universities and the School Board Association to sponsor two follow-up conferences on religion and education, one for school superintendents and the other for school board members. A broad spectrum of issues was considered at each of these well-attended three-day sessions, with speakers representing all viewpoints equally.

Both ADL and NCCJ had two full-time staff-members in Midway. Mr. G., executive director of ADL, is typical of the resourceful and sophisticated leadership enjoyed by these organizations. An absolutist in interpreting of the Court's rulings, he is well informed about the actions of state officials and the rare instances of local controversy. Because of the ADL's lack of a membership base or opportunity for contact with local situations, he has no confirmed knowledge of actual local practices. But from what he knows of other violations of religious freedoms, such as intolerance toward Jehovah's Witnesses and Seventh Day Adventists, he has developed a healthy skepticism about the extent of compliance in Midway schools. And, perhaps because he has no constituency for whose inertia he might bear some responsibility, he was fatalistic but not resentful when confronted with data concerning the extent of schoolhouse religious activity. At one point ADL received a written complaint from several high-school seniors compelled to attend baccalaureate services, but Mr. G. had been unsuccessful in their behalf. This incident was the only occasion, to our knowledge, in which ADL sought to affect local action.

The Parent Teacher Association of Midway is a broadly-inclusive membership organization with wide concern for the operation of the schools but little inclination to seek change in schoolhouse religious practices. Its reactions to the decisions were confined first to a brief tempest over its powers to begin its own conventions and meetings with prayers, and second to a 1964 state convention struggle over a motion to support a constitutional amendment to allow prayer. Despite a contrary recommendation from its Board of Managers, the state convention delegates endorsed the amendment by a narow margin.

The level of interest and controversy within local PTAs concerning the practices of individual schools seems to have been low: the executive secretary of the state association reported that in visits to eighty-four local meetings in the course of two years, she had heard no discussion of the issue. The official interpretation of the Court decisions by the state PTA may have had something to do with this result, of course. Their version was a very narrow one, holding, for example, that recitation of the prayers of Peter Marshall over a school's public address system was not proscribed. The PTA, therefore, was not an organization with unsatisfied or change-oriented goals. It had no impact in the area of schoolhouse religion because it sought none.

But neither did the four civil-libertarian groups—even together—accomplish much in terms of movement toward school practices which would be consistent with the Court's rulings. Why? The basic reason, of course, was the general perception (and, apparently, the fact) of public satisfaction with existing practices, the long-established pattern of teacher-initiated devotional activities, and state officials' personal preferences and disinclination to disturb the "sleeping dogs" of Midway. But more specific reasons are necessary to explain why these attentive and concerned groups undertook no more extensive programs in search of compliance. One factor certainly was the vulnerable nature of all these organizations and their discouraging prior experiences with unpopular causes. The schoolhouse religion issue was not important enough for them—given their established priorities and the multitude of other civil liberties issues and problems which they faced in the Midway context—to make it worth their while to suffer the costs of any serious effort to achieve goals.[3] Realistic assessment of their chances of achieving real compliance suggests that the effort might well have been fruitless in any event—as they apparently assumed—but there is also the possibility that it might have succeeded if they had set about it determinedly, as occurred elsewhere.

Under these circumstances, certain regularities appear within the organizations themselves. None sought to mobilize its membership nor to work through visible legal or other channels, but all contented themselves instead with private lobbying with state officials whose reluctance to act was clear from the start. Although the various executive officials of these interest groups were very well informed about the decisions (including subsequent lower court interpretations) and uniformly strongly supportive, they nevertheless regularly resisted knowledge about local practices inconsistent with those rulings. Apparently, having adjusted to (or rationalized) their inability to secure the results they would have preferred, they found it uncomfortable to acknowledge that reality was so discouraging. In part, the passivity exhibited by most of these organizations ("It's not our job to initiate action; we just wait for complaints") may be owing to the same cause. But these groups were not acting in isolation but in a context of various political forces and expectations in Midway in 1963 and after. We must therefore examine this environment before our understanding of the state-level situation can be complete.

### The Midway Political Context

Whether owing to the preparatory efforts of NCCJ and its

3. And thus political costs are added to money costs to reduce the load of the courts, a "system" fact which cannot be unknown to judges, lawyers, and others who might be involved in court action were all laws to be always enforced. See Lawrence F. Friedman, "Legal Rules and the Process of Social Change," *Stanford Law Review* 19 (June 1967): esp. 798–810.

associates or not, visible statewide reaction to the 1963 decisions was clearly more moderate than in 1962. Quite possibly the 1962 case itself was a sufficient preparatory device, and further Court movement in the same direction became mere confirmation of pessimistic expectations. In any event, state officials and interested groups and organizations had already staked out their positions; they took no special action in response to the 1963 decisions.

By the end of 1963 and the early months of 1964, however, two not unrelated campaigns were getting underway. One was Barry Goldwater's drive for the Republican nomination and then for the presidency. The other was a national campaign for support of a constitutional amendment to authorize some form of prayer in the public schools—a campaign which pushed first the Becker Amendment and then the Dirksen version. Both of these campaigns received enthusiastic support in Midway. Rallies and petition-signing ceremonies regularly joined the two causes. Representative Becker appeared on several occasions to speak at Republican party, American Legion, and other meetings in support of his amendment. Two different national campaigns to collect signatures in support of such an amendment held a series of meetings and rallies at which speakers denounced the Court and called for continued religious observances in the schools. Republican candidates declared themselves in support of the proposed amendments and joined in the denunciation of the Court.[4]

The virulence of these mutually supportive campaigns may account for an otherwise puzzling finding: Midway leaders

4. Actual participation of Midway people in the national controversy over amending the Constitution to permit prayers in the public schools, at least as measured by appearances or submissions before the House Judiciary Committee at hearings on the Becker Amendment, was not great. A total of twelve persons from Midway appeared or submitted statements, eight in favor and four against. Five of the supporters of the amendment were Midway Congressmen (all in favor). The only major opponents of the amendment were one of the capital city newspapers and the Methodist bishop. But interest seems to have been much higher in other states, if this hearing is any measure: nearly 2000 persons appeared or submitted statements, including proportionately much larger delegations from New York and California (both high-compliance states) than from Midway. See U.S. House of Representatives, Committee on the Judiciary, *Hearings Before the Committee on the Judiciary on Proposed Amendments to the Constitution Relating to Prayers and Bible Reading in the Public Schools* (88th Congress, 2d Session, 1964.)

at both state and community levels uniformly viewed school-house religion as a very sensitive issue concerning which there had been great controversy within the state, but at the same time they were unable to specify any local communities where conflict had flared over conforming local practice to Court mandates. Except for the three university towns, where compliance was generally achieved through sustained prodding but without major conflict, and the capital city, where public controversy had led to compliance, no Midway leader could identify a site either of conflict or of systematic compliance. Yet all had images of "sleeping dogs" abounding within the state, ready to awaken if effort were made to achieve compliance. What seems to have developed is a kind of bifurcation: at the level of statewide and national affairs, opposition to the Court and support for both Goldwater and the Republican-sponsored constitutional amendments was loudly and repeatedly proclaimed. But almost no controversy arose over specific practices in the schools of any particular community, so that none of the generalized outrage at the Court or the commitment to religious devotions in the schools found an outlet within a local Midway setting. Thus it became possible for leaders simultaneously to see the issue as highly controversial but to have no actual conflict over a policy change in a Midway school.

There is little doubt that the dominant political ethos of Midway was antithetical to the Court and its ruling on this subject. Any publicly visible effort to induce compliance would probably have served to provide a local focus for much of this bitterness and antipathy. In such circumstances, state officials would probably have been unwilling to act even if they had personally favored the Court's policies. The established associations of school boards and teachers avoided any position-taking on the issue, and even the civil liberties groups were highly circumspect about the manner in which they sought to achieve the changes they endorsed. The elective nature of all of the relevant state officers, including the state superintendent of public instruction, assured that such officers would be sensitive to perceptions of public preferences. At the very least, this sensitivity had the effect of neutralizing the inclination of state-level officials toward law abidance. Left to themselves, or given a prodding by professionals in their midst, the educational officials of the state might have done more to encourage compliance. As it was, they did nothing.

## The Significance of the Overall State-Level Response
## Active Opposition and Passive Support

The reasons for inaction by state-level elites now seem clear. What is more to the point of our inquiry, we have characterized the nature of the cues which came from state officials and other visible guiding bodies. Local elites could be reasonably confident of noninterference with their locally preferred practices, unless a complaint were raised by local initiative. Even then it was not likely that any state-level body would move with alacrity to support the local complaint or to advance it. Any local person inclined to initiate such action would probably have gained the same impressions from a review of the state context and the actions of state officials and groups. Thus, with state official enforcement unlikely, civil liberties groups neutralized, and local complaints discouraged, the field was cleared for local elites and officials to follow locally preferred and established practices. Local decision-makers faced some potentially troublesome questions of personal conscience and political pragmatism, to be sure, but they could be almost totally confident that no outside pressures or actions would shape their behavior. Schoolhouse religious practices, in other words, would be the product exclusively of local decision-making.

We cannot move to our focus on the nature of that local decisional process, however, without noting in summary fashion some of the by-products of this state-level inertia. Although it did not result from or produce intraorganizational tensions—chiefly because it never got that far—the issue of Supreme Court's outlawing of school prayers and Bible reading did induce some curious perceptive and cognitive effects on officials and leaders who held a wide range of views on the merits. In all cases, these effects appear to have been genuine and sincere; we have no reason to believe that they were contrived facades, and accordingly they are the more interesting.

As we have noted, at least two types of transposition emerged. The 1963 decisions were understood to have mandated no more than the *Engel* case's elimination of state-composed prayers, and *Engel* emerged as the basic thrust of the Court's rulings in the area. This permitted an especially narrow view of state responsibility to develop, a view in which the absence of formal school board policy was deemed full compliance with the Court's rulings—despite actual practices in the classroom which were flagrantly violative of *Schempp* and *Murray*. Second, what the Court intended as a cutback in usage of state coercive power (establishment clause grounds) was translated into a Court failure to endorse the religious freedom of majorities to have their teachers say prayers and read the Bible. This permitted special personal emotionalism about one's own religious freedom to be harmonized with opposition to the Court and the elimination of prayer.

We have also seen that practically every leader interviewed at the state level, including those with the most precise and accurate knowledge of the Court's holdings and subsequent lower-court applications, experienced substantial cognitive deflection about actual local practices. This deflection was not owing to the unavailability of information or the surreptitiousness of teachers. The 1964 survey was available, some newspaper reporting was at least adequate, and deep concern would have suggested some effort at inquiry in any event. The better explanation seems to be that compliance (even when thought desirable) was perceived as not very important in the total context of things and quite unlikely in any event, so that great effort in this direction was inappropriate. If nothing was to be done, it would be better not to be too well informed about probable violations of Court policies; any attempt to confront leaders with such evidence was therefore both a threat and a reproach. It was a threat to the organization's reason for existence, because unlimited efforts to achieve compliance could destroy the group's efficacy and influence completely. It was also a threat to the leader's personal accommodation between principle and pragmatism. And it was a reproach to the sincerity and commitment of both leader and organization to the worthy goals for which the group stood. Little wonder then what resentment followed such confrontation.

These perceptual and cognitive effects were observable, as we shall see, in only slightly variant forms at the level of community officials and leaders as well. They appear to be effects rather than causes: it does not seem that state-level elites acted in the way they did because of faulty perceptions or cognitions but because of the interaction of (1) their preferences regarding prayers in the schools with (2) the deep currents of political forces in the state. Once having assumed a particular position with regard to schoolhouse religion (for whatever reasons), these persons' perceptions and cognitions fell into line in such a way as to reduce internal discord and conflict as much as possible. The evidence suggests much the same process at work at the local level, to which we now turn.

# 5 Local
## Elites

# Reactions of
## Inaction

**The Local Settings**

Having seen that the response to the school-prayers decisions at the state level has been a calculated inaction, we
look now to see how Midway's local communities reacted.
The present chapter analyzes responses made by various
members of the educational elite: superintendents of
schools, board members, teachers, and principals. In the
next chapter we will examine the political contexts in which
those responses were made.

We chose to conduct interviews in five communities,
ranging in size from small towns to small cities. Two have
populations of slightly more than 5,000; two are somewhat larger than 10,000; and one has about 45,000 inhab-
itants. All but this latter city are county seats. Population
and industrial diversification have increased steadily
(though not dramatically) during the past two decades
in four of these communities. Business activity in the fifth
is declining somewhat, and employment and the attraction
of new industry are regarded by residents as serious local
problems. Present industries in all five range from agri-

culture to light manufacturing to tourism. Populations in four of the five are strikingly homogeneous; ethnic and racial minorities are virtually absent, though Roman Catholics constitute a minority sizeable enough to support a church in each of the five communities, and two of those churches maintain parochial schools.

The largest of the five cities is distinctive in several ways. It has had a steady influx of laborers from Southern states joining the work force of the variety of light industries built since World War II. It has a small (less than 1 percent of the total) Jewish population, and it is the only one of the cities studied which has a Unitarian Church. With its size and industrial base, moreover, this community is the only one containing more than a local "home grown" elite class; the town claims forty millionaires.

A daily newspaper operates in each place, though typically the four smaller papers devote most of their space to local coverage rather than compete with nearby metropolitan dailies for state, national, or international coverage. Yet all subscribe to and depend heavily upon the wire services.

The structure of local education differs among the five towns in the method of selecting school board members. In two, members are elected; in the others they are appointed by city councils. Each board, however, is composed of representatives from different geographic areas making up the district.

Superintendents in all five communities are full-time professionals, and all possess graduate degrees in education, two having doctorates. Because school district boundaries are considerably broader than the city limits, each having consolidated with surrounding rural areas in the last five years, the population base from which pupils are drawn is much larger than indicated by the size of the town hosting the school. In the case of the two smallest towns, for example, the school population base is four times the size of the town. The superintendents know they are not administering metropolitan systems, but neither do they regard themselves as rural schoolmen. Their "professionalism," as indicated by involvement in state-level educational affairs, is high.

### Community Response to Schempp
The most accurate summary description of these communities' response to the 1962 and 1963 decisions is that they,

like the state of Midway, did nothing. The local school superintendents were certainly aware of the Supreme Court's action, but by their testimony no change in the devotional practices of their schools resulted. Only one had consulted the city attorney for an interpretation of *Schempp,* but the advice he received was apparently to do nothing. In each of the five school systems the prayers and Bible-reading issue was left to the discretion of individual teachers, which means that considerable variation exists. In the same school we found teachers who conducted devotions on a daily basis and others who never had devotions; within the same system we found principals who thought morning prayers and Bible reading were extensively practiced and principals who believed they were extremely rare. In 1967 in one school system the superintendent discovered that one of his elementary teachers listed on the blackboard on Monday the names of her pupils who had attended Sunday school the day before. He asked her to stop this practice, but he would have done so, he said, even in the absence of a *Schempp* decision.

The 1962 *Engel* v. *Vitale* decision, outlawing recitation of a state-composed prayer in New York, was treated in news stories in each of these towns' newspapers. In two of the five, superintendents were quoted as saying that school prayers had been and would continue to be left to the discretion of individual teachers.

Announcement of *Schempp* in early summer, 1963, evoked somewhat less attention in these five newspapers. Coverage was drawn almost exclusively from national wire services, only one paper reporting reactions of local officials. A front page story the day after the Court's ruling ran as follows:

*Recitations Are Used in Local Schools*
Superintendent —— said today recitation of the Lord's Prayer and Bible reading are used in the city schools. He said any teacher from kindergarten through the twelfth grade is permitted to lead a class in the Lord's Prayer if the teacher wants to. He couldn't give an estimate of how often the prayer is used in the schools. The Bible is read . . . in a Bible Literature Course offered to the —— High School students in grades 11 and 12. He said curriculum changes will be made before city schools resume this fall if necessitated by a more specific interpretation of the Supreme Court Ruling.

The same paper carried a story reporting the reactions of local clergymen to *Schempp.* No subsequent stories appeared, however, and the paper never indicated any further announcement by the superintendent or other school official. Superintendents in the other four communities remained silent throughout the episode.

The only school board to discuss the 1963 decision was the one whose superintendent had made a statement to the press. In this case the board agreed with the superintendent's private recommendation to continue to leave the question of devotionals to the judgment of principals and teachers. Boards in the other four communities failed to consider the ruling.

Reaction by persons outside of school officialdom was also rare. Only one superintendent reported having been contacted by any parents, and this followed reports of his statement in the press. PTAs and other community groups normally involved in school affairs expressed nothing in the way of response to *Schempp*. Letters to the editor concerning the issue appeared in only one of the five newspapers, but these were restricted to broadside attacks on the Supreme Court and referred to nothing local.

The evidence is clear that these five Midway communities have done nothing to comply with the decision of the Supreme Court. They have failed, moreover, even to *respond* in any noticeable way. The task of explaining noncompliance in local communities includes, therefore, as it did in the case of state-level action, the task of explaining inertia as well. That task is the problem before us.

### Local Understanding of the Decision

We argued in a previous chapter that the 1963 *Schempp* decision, following by one year the *Engel* v. *Vitale* case, has resulted in a reasonably unambiguous mandate: public schools are not to sponsor devotional exercises in their homerooms during school hours. Fuzzy areas surround this core decision, it is true, leaving ambiguous some continuing practices which courts may some day be compelled to rule on. May baccalaureate services be publicly sponsored affairs, for example? May prayer ever be used in school assemblies or by athletic teams before a game? The Supreme Court, by sending back to Florida courts portions of the *Chamberlain* case, was asking that the terms of disagreement be sharpened before these issues are adjudicated,[1] but on the core issues, resolution has been reached.

The mandate is clear, then, at least in the minds of the Supreme Court justices, many lower courts, and many legal scholars. But is it as clear to the hundreds of thousands of political actors on whose shoulders rests the responsibility of carrying out the mandate? What do teachers, principals, school board members, and especially local school superintendents believe the Court has said? We have just seen how, at the state level in Midway, a number of potentially influential persons have chosen to ignore any mandate to effect changes in schoolhouse religion. A member of the attorney general's staff pleads an inability to understand "those Federal laws"—a gross exaggeration, no doubt, but significant at least in that it points to the *kind* of refuge taken when inaction is desired. The state superintendent of education, assuming that "of course compliance is widespread," fails to compare the new legal standard with the pattern of practices that he must suspect exists, and by so failing, he is implicitly "misunderstanding" the Court's ruling. Many voluntary interest groups in Midway have devoted more time to describing in their newsletters what *is* allowable in the way of religious studies than they have to identifying what is now disallowed.

### Local Elites' Understanding
It would not be surprising, therefore, to discover on the local level a repetition of the state-level misunderstanding of *Schempp*. And, indeed, for all but the superintendents this repetition is found, though there is good reason to believe that local misunderstanding arises not from the sophisticated subterfuge engaged in by state-level elites but from a genuine disinclination to know more about a matter that "obviously doesn't affect us."

Consider the teachers. In each of the five Midway communities, we interviewed classroom teachers, chiefly from the elementary and junior high level. Almost all claimed that they had received no guidelines from principal or superintendent, and, though some denied engaging in any religious exercises whatsoever, the remainder were in a position to

1. See above, p. 29, and see Alexander M. Bickel, *The Least Dangerous Branch* (Indianapolis: Bobbs-Merrill, 1962), chapter 4, for his discussion of the Court's "passive virtues" as devices for ensuring public engagement before decisions are rendered.

compare their own activity with what they understood the
Court to have said.

Miss P., for example, is a second-grade teacher, a veteran
of fifteen years in her school system. Holder of two degrees
and member of the local teachers association and the Na-
·tional Education Association (NEA) as well as the Midway
State Teachers Association, she had nevertheless never heard
of the latter's journal, *The Midway Teacher*. The 1963 decision, she said, "scared us. It means you can pray but you
can't force children to." Moreover, she added, *Schempp*
ruled out anything "sectarian." Miss B., a fifth- and sixth-
grade teacher with nineteen years experience, arrived at a
different conclusion: "You are not supposed to have prayer
in the classroom at all." Mrs. M., of the fourth grade, did
not remember the decision very well: "I think it just elimi-
nates denominationalism or forcing the child to do something
he does not want to do." In her own classroom, therefore,
she is careful not to engage in "denominational" practices,
although, she added, her principal is more cautious. "He's
urged the elimination of opening prayers at school-wide
assemblies."

Some image of distance along a primrose path appears
in the thoughts of Mrs. V., a kindergarten teacher. A two-
year veteran with a B.A. degree and a consultant for Midway's Headstart program, Mrs. V. said that, to her knowledge,
her school system has no policy on prayer: "Just don't go
too far." She therefore uses silent meditation and group
prayer because it "relaxes" the children, teaching them
respect and reverence. "It has a value sharing function in
the classroom."

What might be going on in the head of Mrs. G., a second-
grade teacher, is difficult to say. With absolutely no group
affiliation anymore outside of her school because of an
invalid mother, Mrs. G., a thirteen-year veteran, told us,
"I just accepted the fact that they weren't going to allow
prayer. Before the decision I used to say the prayer and
the pledge every morning; now I just pledge." However,
this change did not disturb her: "We don't get very upset
about this sort of thing here." The reasons no doubt can
be found in what she estimates *Schempp* still allows. In the
interviewer's words:

She may not have prayers every morning, but she does just
about every other thing religious one could think of. She

has Sunday school charts up on her walls, and the kids get
stars for every time they go to Sunday School, racing to see
who can get the most stars. She tells Christmas and Easter
stories, and the children make Nativity scenes during Christmas
time. She encourages them not only to go to Sunday school
but also to tell her on Monday mornings that they went, whom
they saw there, and so on. She says she talks a lot in class
about the importance of church. She thinks religious training
is extremely important, and this is something she has a responsibility for in the school; this is her contribution. "I'm not
able to be at the church anymore, but I feel I compensate
by what I do in school."

Mrs. L. is a similar case. Elderly, with forty-two years
experience, she is a former Sunday school teacher in the
local Methodist church, and her public school classroom must
seem little different: "I consider it my professional responsibility to teach children religion." To this end (according
to the interviewer's notes again) her students

start off every morning with a morning prayer and they start
off every afternoon with an afternoon prayer, and they say
grace before they have lunch. They sing Sunday school songs
in the afternoon, and Mrs. L. encourages them to learn new
songs on Sunday in order to teach their classmates. She encourages pupils also to bring other Sunday school material
so it can be used in class and put up on the wall. She reads
Bible stories every afternoon, but in addition she makes use of
*Wee Wisdom,* a child's religious magazine. The prayers and
religious poems in *Wee Wisdom* are taught so they can be
recited. Mrs. L. says she's always been a little disappointed that
none of her third graders ever wanted to lead the class in
their own spontaneous prayers, so the class says prayers
learned at home, at Sunday school, or from *Wee Wisdom.* She
tells them the Christmas and Easter stories, starting "real
early with the Easter story because it is not just the Resur-
rection—there is an awful lot that goes before it."

When asked whether she thought her practice might not
be excessive, Mrs. L. noted that she had had no directive
from anybody. The teachers association? "They worry about
things like getting a shorter lunch hour." The PTA? "They
are involved in donating silverware to the cafeteria or shrub-
bery to the school grounds." The superintendent, she says,
has said nothing about praying or not praying. Meanwhile,
"You know, in many ways this is the only chance that some
of these children get to hear about religion."

More is involved here, of course, than mere failure to understand the intent of the Court's ruling. Decisions are received not by a *tabula rasa,* to make their independent impressions, but always by a mind already filled with bits of knowledge, preference for practices, and predispositions to respond in various ways. Moreover, each cluttered mind receives its message not independently but in a context of other minds. Teachers report that few of these "other minds" helped them in formulating a reaction to *Schempp,* but it is instructive to investigate why.

### Principals' Understanding
Teachers told us that few if any directives came from principals; principals confirmed the fact by telling us they sent few if any. One of the major reasons why principals issued no orders on schoolhouse religion, they said, is because there was no need to. And they felt no need to, it is quite clear, because in part they did not fully understand what the Court had outlawed. Let us illustrate.

Mr. D. is nearing retirement, having spent twenty-five years in his county as principal of one or another school. He is a "mainstay" in his Baptist church, he said, and most of his extraschool activity revolves around things religious. Personally opposed to prayers in public schools ("It's dangerous; a Jehovah's Witness could get you in a lot of trouble if you tried"), Mr. D. has nevertheless supplied his teachers with no guidelines because nothing illegal goes on to his knowledge. The Bible can still be read, as far as he knows, "but a teacher just can't comment on it." However, it is his belief that Bible reading does not occur in the classrooms of his school although, interestingly enough, he is the president of his community's Gideon Society, whose chief task is distributing Bibles in the public schools.

Principal L. has a somewhat more focused view of the *Schempp* decision. The Court, he says, has outlawed prayer and Bible reading "if the children don't want it." The school's obligation is to the parents in the neighborhood it serves. As far as he is aware, this interpretation is that of his superintendent, too. Indeed, the superintendent's wife has recently taught in Mr. L.'s school, and she read Bible stories to her pupils.

Mr. M., another elementary school principal, does not see how religion can be omitted, even in disciplinary matters.

The Court decision means that the Bible cannot be interpreted in the classroom; teachers are not to inject their own beliefs. Mr. M. admits to a certain confusion about the legal refinements of *Schempp,* but of this he is certain: "Being sectarian in the classroom is definitely off base." Prayer also is out; nobody is to pray in school, but "all teachers do something in the way of religion."

The policy of principal O. is to leave religious practices up to his teachers' discretion. "They have a free hand here." No fuss has been created, so he has felt no need to elaborate on that policy. The Supreme Court ruling, he said, applied to New York and any other states with prescribed prayers. In this understanding of the pair of decisions, Mr. O. is joined by Mr. W. in still another community. Prayers written by school authorities and required in the entire school system are outlawed, he said, but he tells teachers to do as they want. He guessed that perhaps half of the teachers in his building have daily prayer or Bible reading.

It would be a mistake to assume from these comments that principals (or teachers) simply fail to grasp the real meaning of the Supreme Court's decisions and thus permit the range of religious practices they do permit. Our documentation here is not to support the argument that the law is being broken in many classrooms because of teachers' and principals' confusion or ignorance. After all, our respondents could have been falsifying their testimony or, more likely, could be explaining implicit policy which pervades their school systems. Our purpose is rather to show by these few cases (we could have cited other similar ones) that, whatever is the community's schoolhouse religion policy, lower-authority personnel are unlikely to challenge it on legal grounds. Teachers, we saw, are quite vague about the Court's mandate; principals, we now see, are at best only a little clearer.

### The Executive Level

Had teachers and principals merely been rationalizing a policy which they knew countermanded a Supreme Court ruling, one of the likely sources of such a policy would have been the school boards in these communities. Each of the Midway towns we investigated participates in a consolidated school district governed by a seven- or five-man board. We were able to interview sixteen of the thirty-one board

members and quiz them on their understanding of *Schempp*.
Though they varied in many ways, these men can summarily
be described as disinterested in the implications of *Schempp*
for their schools and disinclined to discover what religious
practices occur therein. For example, none gave evidence
of having read the decision, and, though there was disagreement as to whether religious practices should have
been outlawed, no one felt any need to enunciate a policy
or even find out what current practice was. Significantly,
those who agreed with the 1963 ruling generally assumed
compliance in their districts; those who disagreed generally
assumed noncompliance; and those who understand nothing
of the *Schempp* decision could not guess the extent to which
prayer and Bible reading occurred.

Mr. S., an executive in an industrial corporation in his
town, claimed "no real understanding" of the Court ruling,
but said that it was the law and should be obeyed. To his
knowledge *Schempp* was obeyed by the schools in his area
(which is not true), in part because the school attorney
rendered an interpretation of *Schempp* (which, the attorney
said, he never did). Board member H., an engineer for a
regional power company, said that the Supreme Court had
ruled out "official prayers" and that schools in his jurisdiction did not have official prayers. In any event, however,
"Just because it's national policy doesn't mean we have to
do it." Teachers, he told the superintendent, should be allowed to continue doing what they have been doing. Mr. M.,
in contrast to the others, did not care one way or the other.
A middle-aged skilled worker, Mr. M. recalled a sermon by
his Methodist minister which condemned the Court decision,
and he himself is "generally anti-Court," but he has engaged
in no discussion on the Board or elsewhere about *Schempp,*
it being "only minor" compared to other decisions the Supreme Court has handed down. People in his community,
Mr. M remarked, "don't really care enough about it to try
to bring a change." A change from *what* he could not say.

Almost to a man, however, these school board members
told us something else which helps to explain their disinterest
in and disinclination to act on schoolhouse religion. Such
matters, they claimed, are properly handled by the superintendent of schools. Financial policy is their domain, but
educational policy is set by the professionals they hire. How,

then, have superintendents understood the Court's action on prayers and Bible reading?

## The Educational Cosmopolites

At the apex of local school affairs is the superintendent of schools. As has been mentioned, the largest of the cities we investigated has a population of only 45,000 or so, but the school districts of which the towns are a part are, owing to consolidation, much larger. The administrative heads of these districts are appropriately involved, therefore, in manifold activities within but also without their local communities. All belong to national, state, and regional associations whose purposes are to expand members' administrative capacity. All receive many journals and newsletters aimed at helping them with budgets, personnel, and curriculum. And all attend periodic conferences and conventions, on which occasions they engage formally and informally in discussions of how to run schools and, not least, how to get federal funds. Each of them, moreover, is assisted by one or more assistant superintendents who help in administering the policies of their districts. Though parochial in some ways, the superintendents are thus remarkably cosmopolitan in the educational arena. Vidich and Bensman describe the corresponding person in their small town of Springdale as the "alien expert."[2] With perhaps less emphasis on the word alien, the label also fits these Midway superintendents.

Expert indeed, but alien only in the sense that their mobility is greater than that of teachers, principals, or board members, all five of these superintendents are heavily involved in wider community affairs. At least three of the five are or have been members of their local church governing boards, including two who served as chairmen. Service club membership (usually Rotary or Kiwanis) is common, and one spoke of his country club membership. Other activities such as Boy Scouts and welfare programs also occupy their leisure time.

It is clear that all five are well positioned to hear the community sentiment, at least from those whose sentiment matters. Superintendent F. told us that after only four years in

2. Arthur J. Vidich and Joseph Bensman, *Small Town in Mass Society* (Princeton, New Jersey: Princeton University Press, 1958), p. 190.

town he not only knew his present board members well but
also he knew all the persons who were likely ever to be
elected to his board. But this communication channel flows
both ways; our five respondents use elaborate devices to
keep board members and other citizens informed. Mr. C.,
for example, welcomes the local newspaper editor, a personal friend, to school board meetings, but nevertheless Mr.
C. or an assistant writes the news copy which the paper
publishes. This superintendent went so far as to study the
local paper's style so the editing of his copy would be minimal. Superintendent O. opened his desk drawer to show
us a stack of stamped envelopes already addressed to his
board members; any time a message to them comes to mind,
he said, he jots it down and mails it right out. Two of
Superintendent O.'s four board members, all of whom we
interviewed, volunteered that he sent "too much" material for
them to digest. This board, incidentally, meets not only in
periodic public sessions but also for private luncheons and
on social occasions. Mr. C., on the other hand, avoids
social contact with his members because he wants to preclude any taint of collusion. He even broke off a friendship
by mutual agreement after the friend was elected to the
school board. Yet, his board members explained, they receive two or three telephone calls a week from Mr. C.

Masters of communication then and, above all, expert
educational politicians, these superintendents are obviously
key persons in setting and carrying out school policy. What
do they know about the meaning of *Schempp*?

**Messages Sent and Messages Received**
We have seen already that the local daily newspapers in
these five Midway communities carried newswire stories of
the 1962 and 1963 decisions. If more attention was given
to the first ruling, which had direct impact only for New
York State, the papers were merely following the national
pattern; throughout the United States *Engel* v. *Vitale* raised
more public outcry than did *Schempp*.[3] But it would be an
error to assume that superintendents of schools anywhere
were given little information on the implications of the 1963
decision. Radio and TV, of course, were other sources of

3. Johnson, *The Dynamics of Compliance*, pp. 79–90.

information, as were popular magazines.[4] And in addition to mass media discussion, a number of journals specifically aimed at school administrators carried articles about *Schempp* as well as about the New York Regents' Prayer case.[5] The American Association of School Administrators commissioned an eight-member task force to

examine the effect of recent decisions of the Supreme Court on the issues of Bible reading and prayer in the public schools. The charge further called upon us to suggest constructive means by which public school administrators could guide the development of local policies and practices, responding to the Court's interpretation of the Constitution on this subject.

The task force's report, *Religion in the Public Schools,* was published a year later.[6]

It is not surprising, then, to find that, on the legal question of schoolhouse religion, superintendents were relatively better informed than teachers, principals, or school board members. Several indicated to us that they had read the two decisions of 1962 and 1963, and the *McCollum* and *Zorach* cases, dealing a decade earlier with released-time religious instruction, were not unknown to them. "Better informed" in this instance, however, means only that these men had read more and thought more about *Schempp*; it does not mean their understanding necessarily coincided more with the Supreme Court's intent or with subsequent court interpretation. Actually, the five superintendents differed a little in what they believed is allowed and disallowed.

Superintendent C. is probably most accurate in his understanding of *Schempp,* largely because he happened to take a course in school law soon after the 1963 decision. Students have a right not to be "captives at prayer," he said, and since social pressures make it difficult or impractical for

4. Using the *Reader's Guide to Periodical Literature* for the period June 1962 to June 1964, Shettle found "roughly two hundred" items pertaining to the prayer cases (Carolyn Shettle, "An Analysis of Public Opinion on the Supreme Court Prayer Decision Cases," M.A. thesis, Department of Sociology, University of Wisconsin, 1967).

5. For example, Johnson, *The Dynamics of Compliance,* pp. 90–94, cites nine articles in four journals of educational administration appearing between July 1962 and October 1963.

6. American Association of School Administrators, *Religion in the Public Schools* (Washington, D.C., 1964). The quotation is from p. v.

objecting pupils to get up and leave, the Court has ruled that schools may not sponsor such practices. A number of teachers in his district do, however, engage in prayer and/or Bible reading in their classrooms, and Mr. C. is aware of that. Indeed, incoming teachers are encouraged by their principals, at the superintendent's direction, to have devotional exercises. The teacher handbook indicates as much, though it also indicates that an instructor may choose not to. Mr. C. estimated that perhaps 50 percent of his elementary teachers engage in such practices.

Superintendent O. sees *Schempp* as ruling out "sectarianism"; no particular religion should be fostered, but celebration of "our cultural heritage" is permitted. In effect, then, schools in the same system but in different neighborhoods may engage in different kinds of religious practices. Baccalaureate services, for example, have thus been stopped because Jews and Catholics objected to the "Protestant" service. Even though attendance was voluntary, objecting students were paying social penalties, and this made the baccalaurate service unacceptable. Similarly, a teacher who was discovered to be distributing Sunday school literature in her classroom was asked to desist; that activity was sectarian and "beyond the pale." Aware that others have interpreted *Schempp* to mean no religious practice is allowed, Mr. O. claimed that such an interpretation is inconsistent with what the Court really said. The Court is not really "anti-religion," and neither is Mr. O. He is unaware of any "illegal" practices in his schools, therefore, but if he finds any he will stop them. About a third of his elementary classrooms, our interviewing revealed, have devotional exercises.

The other three superintendents we interviewed express minor variations of a "voluntaristic" interpretation of *Schempp*: If no coercion is applied, then any practice is alright. Superintendent G. stated that just as it is unconstitutional for the state of Midway to require religious exercises, so it is illegal for a local school board or a local superintendent or a principal to require them. But individual teachers may be given the option of leading prayers or Bible reading. Interestingly, Mr. G. suspects that the high school baccalaureate service, a graduation exercise which for reasons of size has moved from rotating local churches back into the school auditorium, may be found to be unconstitutional because it is school sponsored and mandatory. But the grace before lunch, a practice in which many of his teachers engage, is, in Mr. G.'s understanding, consonant with the Court ruling.

Superintendent F. not only permits but also approves of prayer and Bible reading in his teachers' classrooms. His community, he explained, wants such things, and the Supreme Court was referring to places where such things are not wanted. Mr. F., however, makes it clear that in these matters teachers are free to conduct their classrooms in whatever manner they prefer. Coercion, in other words, is not employed.

Finally, Superintendent A. expresses his voluntarism principle in similar ways. The school attorney, he told us, is called in for writing contracts or land negotiation, but when it comes to interpreting the Supreme Court rulings, Mr. A. himself feels qualified. And his interpretation? The Court outlawed coercion. "And since we don't coerce, no change on our part is called for." Mr. A. suspects that little in the way of morning devotionals goes on anyway, though pre-lunch grace is widely used, he said. Moreover, the Hi-Y clubs in the high school sponsor morning broadcasts over homeroom loudspeakers, and these, we were told, will sometimes contain prayers or Bible reading. A teacher who recorded on Monday her pupils' Sunday school attendance of the previous day was told to stop; she was being coercive. But when representatives of the local ministerial association consulted him about the feasibility of periodic devotional assemblies in the high school, Mr. A.'s response was to tell them to present a plan. That a plan never came forth pleased the superintendent, but apparently because he does not think very highly of the ministers, not because he felt the practice would be illegal.

### A Search for an Explanation

An explanation is obviously needed. Here is a variety of school personnel, in a variety of towns, with various interpretations of two Supreme Court rulings having considerable implications for their behavior—and yet with only minor exceptions no change in their schoolhouse religion has come about. Why? It is clear that these Midway communities *might* have complied; we saw in an earlier chapter that compliance with *Schempp* is no rare phenomenon. The question is why, unlike many other school personnel elsewhere in the nation, the educators in these five towns felt no need to change their behavior with respect to school prayer and Bible reading.

One possible answer might have been found at the state level. Agencies "above" these communities, from the governor to the legislature and from the attorney general to the state superintendent, could have ordered a stop to schoolhouse religion, in which case compliance would likely have been forthcoming. Or these agencies could have advocated no change, in which case the fact of noncompliance would cease to be a puzzling feature of towns and would become a feature of the state, to be explained. But Midway, we saw in the previous chapter, did nothing as a state about *Schempp,* thus suggesting that the action (or inaction) of these five communities must be explained by characteristics of the communities themselves. And since the local superintendents play so strategic a role in their communities' educational affairs, it is likely to be around them that we shall find the explanation.

One answer can be disposed of immediately. It is *not* the case that these superintendents were unaware of the Supreme Court's rulings on school prayers and Bible reading. Other actors in the educational arena had varying degrees of knowledge about *Engel* v. *Vitale* and *Schempp,* but the superintendents, we have just seen, were perfectly aware of those decisions, had access to much information about them, and understood that there was at least the possibility that changes were called for. So the noncompliance we have observed is not owing to the fact that superintendents failed to know about the rulings.

Two other general possibilities exist, however. First, it may be that, though superintendents (and even other educational elites) know about *Schempp,* they do not approve of it. And second, whether or not they happen to agree with *Schempp,* the rewards for complying may be far outweighed by the penalties. We shall discuss next the first of these points, saving the second for a following chapter.

### Nonresponse and Noncompliance

To judge from its publication of a special commission report, the American Association of School Administrators approved the Supreme Court's decisions in *Engel* v. *Vitale* and *Schempp.*

The Commission . . . accepts and supports the decisions of the Supreme Court respecting prayer and Bible reading in the public schools of the nation. . . . The Commission properly assumes that school administrators themselves give full allegiance and prompt obedience to the law, notwithstanding the fact that many leaders in politics, in the press, and even in religious bodies may appear to advocate defiance of the law.[7]

Had the school administrators to whom we talked shared the convictions of the AASA, then either they would have made efforts to bring their schools' practices into line with Court rulings, or else they would likely have exhibited considerable anguish over their failure to do so. But the five superintendents (plus everyone else we talked to in their communities) gave evidence of neither.

Contrast this situation with Johnson's discussion of the school superintendent in Eastville-Westville, a rural school system in Illinois that *did* comply.

To the . . . superintendent, the Court's rulings on religious practices in public schools were "right," expressive of his own values. . . . He applied a rather rigid standard of constitutionality. . . . The prayer before lunch in the school cafeterias was interpreted by him to be an "establishment of religion." . . . His response to the imbalance (of law and behavior) was to change the ongoing behavior. On three occasions he informally mentioned to the principals of the elementary schools that the practice of formal prayer before lunch should be stopped. . . . Finally in a . . . teachers' meeting his position was stated to the principals and teachers alike. . . . This more formal articulation of the superintendent's expectations brought the desired compliance.[8]

Johnson, of course, is not to be interpreted here as asserting that compliance came about simply because the superintendent wished it. Nor are we to be interpreted as implying that compliance did not come about in the Midway communities simply because their superintendents did *not* wish it. Such matters typically are not one man's decision but rather are embedded in a decision-making context. Johnson makes that context very clear in the case of Eastville-Westville;

7. Ibid, pp. 8.
8. Johnson, *The Dynamics of Compliance,* pp. 106–7.

we hope to do the same in our next chapter in the case of the five Midway localities. What we are asserting here is the importance of superintendents' views of the Court and its rulings, if not for the final outcome in a given instance involving a Court-related issue, then at least for their orientation toward this decision-making context.[9] That these five superintendents not only failed to initiate changes in the direction of compliance but also failed to evidence any concern about the issue is a question of some importance, therefore, and requires further discussion.

It might be expected that, as well-educated leaders, school superintendents in general are quite favorably disposed toward the United States Supreme Court.[10] Such a statement does not mean, of course, that leaders approve of all decisions handed down by the Court; indeed, their generalized approval of the Court as an institution is accompanied by a heightened critical sense as well, so that leaders more than the public-at-large are likely to have strong reactions to specific decisions. But it does mean that superintendents of schools are probably going to have a "benevolent" or trusting view of the judicial branch, seeing it, more than the public sees it, as "neutral," "fair," and concerned with the nation's welfare.

Our interviewing in Midway would confirm this point of view, not only of superintendents but of other educational elites and community leaders also. Considering the volatility of the prayer and Bible-reading issue in the nation as a whole, we unearthed only one comment that could be construed as the least bit negative toward the Court, and that, coming from a rural school board member, was very mild. He is, he said, generally "anti-Court." The superintendents, however, evidenced not even that little bit of hostility. Surely their noncompliance and nonresponse to the issues in *Schempp* arise not from any antipathy for the Court's legitimacy, not from any challenge to its right to make legal decisions. But perhaps, in spite of a generalized approval of the

9. William K. Muir, Jr., *Religion in the Public Schools* (Chicago: University of Chicago Press, 1967), is a clear demonstration of the variety of orientations school personnel may have on this issue.
10. See above, chapter 2, tables 4 and 5. Leaders in the research reported there refer to newspaper editors, clergymen, and political party county chairmen, not school superintendents, so the "expectation" of favorable disposition remains just that—an expectation.

Court as an institution, these school administrators happened
to disapprove of this specific decision. Would they then
not reveal a certain hesitancy about complying, and might
not this hesitancy manifest itself not only in noncompliance
but in nonresponse as well? Given our methods of inquiry we
cannot rule out such a possibility, to be sure, but it can
be pointed out that, again with the exception of a very few
school board members, not a hostile word was spoken against
the *Schempp* decision. It just does not seem to be the case
that the educators to whom we spoke viewed with alarm
the elimination of school-sponsored prayers and Bible reading. The amount of affect they *personally* invested in the
issue was simply not great. Were all their religious practices
somehow magically (and, more importantly, without controversy) to disappear, we surmise that these five superintendents, a good number of their teachers and principals, and
even their school boards would not have been deeply
troubled.

Why, then, were efforts to obey the 1963 decision not
forthcoming? One answer, we think, lies in the schoolman's
adoption of voluntarism, a principle which was revealed
earlier in our discussion of educators' understanding of the
Court's decisions, but a principle needing greater elabora-
tion here.

**Establishment versus Free Exercise**
Mr. Justice Black, writing for the majority in the 1962 *Engel*
v. *Vitale* case, said:

Neither the fact that the [Regents] prayer may be denomina-
tionally neutral, nor the fact that its observance on the
part of students is voluntary can serve to free it from the
limitations of the Establishment Clause, *as it might from the
Free Exercise Clause,* of the First Amendment.[11]

Schoolmen, committed as they are to the voluntarism
element in the American political culture, failed to grasp
the meaning of this accented phrase, we would assert, and
as a result they found it difficult to regard what they were
doing as illegal, unconstitutional, or immoral. Let us explain.
The mass media treated the two school-prayers cases to

11. *Engel* v. *Vitale,* 370 U.S. 421 (June 1962). Italics added. Mr.
Justice Clark, for the majority in *Abington* v. *Schempp* in 1963,
wrote in a similar fashion.

a large extent as if they indicated an anti-religious Court.[12]
Many persons (including Mr. Justice Clark in a speech a
month after *Engel v. Vitale*) therefore felt compelled to
assure the public that antireligion was not the Court's motive,
and elimination of all signs of religion in public schools
was not its intent. Where Black, writing the majority opinion
in *Engel v. Vitale,* had relegated to a footnote a disclaimer
of the Court's antireligiousness, Clark, in *Schempp,* took
occasion more than once to indicate that religious studies,
including study of the Bible as literature, were entirely
within legal bounds.

The upshot in many locales was a debate over the tangential question of the *amount* of religion allowed by the Court
when, in fact, the core issue revolved around the issue of
establishment versus free exercise of religion in public schools.
The Supreme Court, though stating that school-sponsored
devotional exercises are an "establishment" of religion, was
interpreted frequently as meaning that schools could not
abridge pupils' "free exercise" of religion, including their
freedom *not* to participate in religious devotionals. The denominational neutrality and voluntary nature of the New
York Regents Prayer might have freed it from the limitations of the free exercise clause but not from those of the
establishment clause, as Black wrote. But a significant number
of educational elites in Midway apparently did not grasp
this distinction. The Court, as they understood it, was re-
asserting that crucial element in the American political
culture: The state shall not require religious exercises; the
state shall respect religious diversity; and therefore its public
schools shall protect the religious rights of all students.

There is good reason to believe that the superintendents
with whom we talked—and not just superintendents but
everyone else in Midway who is concerned about schools—
are thoroughly committed to this "religious voluntarism"
aspect of the American culture.

We have already seen how pervasive is the educational
elite's belief that denominationalism, sectarianism, forcing
children, interpreting the Bible according to one's own beliefs,
or "going beyond the pale" in religious exercises is inappropriate in public schools. It is interesting to see that, when
confronted by *Engel v. Vitale* and *Schempp,* therefore, these

12. Johnson, *The Dynamics of Compliance,* chap. 6; William A.
Hachten, "Journalism and the Prayer Decision."

persons interpreted the Court as having outlawed "coercive" or "official" religious practices. Establishment to them, in other words, is not at issue; free exercise is. But since in "our" schools, nobody's freedom of religious exercise is threatened—

Each of the superintendents was adamant in denying that his district coerced students or teachers in the matter of religious exercises. No district had promulgated any official prayers, none called for devotionals of any kind, and none had an explicit policy. Teacher interviews confirmed such testimony; we found no faculty member who could remember ever receiving directions on whether and how to conduct classroom devotionals. One teachers' handbook explicitly stated that teachers were free to follow their own preferences in this regard, and one superintendent had written his high-school principal that Hi-Y morning broadcasts (which sometimes include devotional elements) are legal and are to continue. But apart from these two official acts, we found evidence only of administrative silence on schoolhouse religion.

Reasons given for the silence reveal how strongly the notion of religious freedom is held. Superintendent E. sees divisiveness in schools as the sign that freedom is being curtailed. Certainly, he said, if someone objected to a particular religious practice, he would end it. For example, Thanksgiving, Christmas, and Easter are now celebrated in his public schools. "In some neighborhoods" these practices might be found objectionable, in which case Mr. E. would order them stopped. But nobody has objected yet, so they may continue.

Superintendent G. takes a similar view. If his schools tried to do more in the way of religion, he told us, some people would object. Since there has been no complaint, however, it is apparent to Mr. G. that no person's religious freedom is threatened. Superintendent F. understands the doctrine of case law to mean not only that his school system would individually have to be sued if religious exercises were to be eliminated but also that, unless a suit is brought in his community, he can assume that persons regard their religious freedom as protected.

An incident occurring during an interview with a school board member illustrates nicely how the American political culture can mask the distinction between establishment and

free exercise. Mr. H., a farmer, represents a rural area
which in recent years has consolidated with the city schools.
Upon being asked what practices went on in his district's
schools, he pleaded ignorance but called over his hired hand's
fifth-grade daughter and asked if she ever had Bible readings
in class. She said she did not but that her school had
"periodic chapel" conducted by one or another area Protestant minister. "Do teachers tell students they do not have
to go if they don't want to?" asked Mr. H. The girl answered
no. "Does a Catholic priest or a rabbi ever conduct the
service?" was the next question. Again the girl said no, to
which Mr. H. responded, "Well, we'll change that!"

One anecdote does not an argument make, we readily
agree, but viewed in the context of frequent comments about
how "we don't force anybody here" and "we respect everybody's religion," Mr. H.'s comprehension of *Schempp* as a
free exercise–based decision is tellingly revealed in his con-
versation. And in this respect, we would claim, he is not
unlike other Midway citizens involved in educational affairs.
The schoolman mentality, with its accent on voluntarism or
freedom, finds it difficult to grasp the notion of establishment. If everyone is free and everything is voluntary and
nobody complains, then what could possibly be unconstitutional?

### Schoolmen and Nonresponse

Noncompliance in these Midway communities cannot be
explained, of course, simply by reference to the educational
elite's failure to distinguish between establishment and free
exercise. This failure is strongly related to the elite's nonresponse, however, and thus is indirectly relevant to the
fact of little or no change in their schoolhouse religion
practices—the inertia in Midway. For example, Superintendent O., when confronted by the interviewer's suggestion
that his schools were "Protestant parochial," understood quite
well what was meant by the phrase. He and his assistant
administrator have in fact discussed exactly that issue, he
said. But their discussion, it is clear, is over the degree
to which schools may legitimately be Protestant in their
parochialism, not over whether schools should be parochial
in this sense. Since the great majority of pupils are Protestant, and since non-Protestants have their rights respected

and have raised no objections, the issue seems resolved to Superintendent O.'s satisfaction.

Mr. Justice Douglas, several years after *Schempp,* published a book outlining his reasons for concurring in the Court's schoolhouse religion decisions. "Once public school prayers are the prize," he wrote, "a bitter contest is on for control of the school board. Only those who have gone through that political experience know the full depth and power of religious animosities."[13] Our respondents simply have not gone through "that political experience" over school prayer. Were they to do so, they would without question try to uphold the principles of voluntarism and pluralism— that is their mentality as schoolmen—but in the meantime, with no bitter contest in sight, devotional prayers and Bible reading remain nonissues to which a nonresponse is entirely appropriate.

Such is not the way with all nonissues, of course. In one of these five communities, the superintendent has instituted a "controversial issues" program into the curriculum, complete with a guidelines book, publicity, and a willingness to defend it against the forces of opposition. In another, the superintendent and his board are carefully laying the several years of groundwork in preparation for sex education in the schools. Schoolmen do not dodge controversy simply because it is controversial, in other words. And that is why their nonresponse to *Schempp,* their disinterest in schoolhouse religion as an issue, has required an explanation. Not that, had they been so inclined, superintendents necessarily could unilaterally have eliminated prayers and Bible reading. School policy decisions seldom are unilaterally made and carried out; they tend to be embedded in a context of decisions and persons, of values and issues.

13. William O. Douglas, *The Bible and the Schools* (Boston: Little, Brown and Co., 1966), p. 47.

# 6 The Local Context

## A Setting for Avoidance

**Local Educational Affairs in Historicopolitical Perspective**

In his report on the impact of the 1952 *Zorach* decision, in which released-time religious instruction was permitted with the provision that it occur off school property, Sorauf suggested that

> a Supreme Court precedent is in no sense an objective fact, that its interpretations and applications depend as much on the goals and involvements of the groups concerned as on the words of the decision itself. To rephrase the old saw, the precedent in reality consists of what influential partisans and decision-makers say the Supreme Court says it is.[1]

The key phrases here are, of course, "goals and involvements" and "influential partisans and decision-makers." The first suggests that Supreme Court (or any) directives to communities are received always in a context which itself is already filled with political issues, alignments, and battlegrounds. The second suggests that in this political context, some contestants are more strategic than others in determining a

1. Sorauf, *"Zorach* v. *Clauson,"* pp. 790–91.

directive's outcome. Compliance (or, in the present instance, noncompliance) is to be understood, then, in terms of the setting in which the directive arrives and of the response to that directive by certain power wielders in the setting. This generalization is as true of a Supreme Court decision as of any other. And it is as true of a decision mediated through, for example, state agencies as of one which calls for direct action on the local level. Differences emerge only with respect to which political issues in the setting are "activated" and who among the power wielders get involved.

In our continued analysis of how Midway school districts could fail to comply with the intentions of the *Schempp* decision, we therefore turn to these two issues: first, we investigate the historicopolitical contexts of the five local communities; and, second, we discuss the matter of who holds local power and how they wield it. By implication at least, a third issue thus emerges: the ineffectiveness of those without power.

## The Magnetism of Historicopolitical Contexts

Each of the superintendents to whom we talked used the term *power structure*. For these educational cosmopolites, in other words, school administration is accurately seen as *political* maneuvering. Each superintendent confronts a web of interests and power to which he reacts and on which he acts. Self-defined success as a superintendent thus becomes a matter of his capacity to pursue his educational goals with the minimum strain in this web of interests. Not surprisingly, occasions arise when placating the power structure takes precedence over the attainment of educational goals. But at least to the superintendents in this study, a do-nothing, caretaker tenure is not the model to be followed. Indeed, it is only on some kinds of issues that such a path can be followed. The web of interests itself contains some elements which are pushing and some which are pulling; superintendent inertia is therefore a rarity, even when it is sought.

The term historicopolitical context refers, then, to those continuing, magnetic issues which draw to themselves and help to define all other issues. Political alignments on any new issue, for example, will tend to form along the lines of old issues, and enmities and interests from previous battles will tend to structure subsequent battles. The historico-political context for educational affairs of course overlaps—

indeed in some cases may be identical with—the contexts for other political affairs in the community.[2] But the degree of overlap differs according to a number of factors—whether school board elections are partisan races, for example, or whether school building results in property-tax increases or is conducted in some other manner. In any event, our point is a simple one, though profound in its consequences: any proposed alteration in the school system will occur against a backdrop of the web of interests we are calling a historico-political context. Though our superintendents referred to this phenomenon not by that term but in its present mani-festation as power structure, they nevertheless knew very well its identity and its meaning.

This historicopolitical context for educational affairs can vary from community to community. In one, the decline of agriculture and concomitant efforts to commercialize will intrude into every school issue.[3] In another, ethnic mixing may predominate. In still another, suburban location with its commuter population may get involved in all school affairs. Chapter 3 above provides a hint that some commun-ities in America's Bible Belt may find their educational issues revolving around Protestant orthodoxy, whereas it is clear that in, say, metropolitan Boston, Protestant orthodoxy is unlikely to be a pervasive political force.

### Basketball and Consolidation

The Midway communities we investigated exhibited remark-ably similar historicopolitical contexts for educational affairs. They are all relatively small as cities go (ranging, it will be recalled, from about 5,000 to something over 45,000 popu-lation), and no doubt their size has something to do with their homogeneity in this regard. But in addition: (1) they are still feeling the effects of a postwar baby boom; (2) they are in a state which in the last decade has pushed for con-solidation of school districts; and (3) they are part of an area where, as one clergyman told us, "basketball is a reli-gion." These three characteristics combine to form a historico-

2. Thus, in Springdale, a small rural town in upper New York State, the school board is "politically . . . the area in which most community issues, interest, activities and discussion are present" (Vidich and Bensman, *Small Town in Mass Society,* p. 175).
3. As it apparently does in Springdale. Ibid. Chap. 7 describes how budgets, curriculum, personnel, i.e., virtually every educational matter, reflects the rural-urban division.

political context for educational affairs which, like a magnet, has drawn the school-prayers issue to itself, shaped it as a local issue, and greatly determined its present status. Let us elaborate.

As with almost every other city and hamlet, Midway's communities have experienced a baby boom during the last two decades. Though the populations of the five towns we studied have experienced unequal growth, with one growing not at all, each has increased in its proportion of school age children. More important even than such natural growth in pupil population, though, has been the growth resulting from school district consolidation. As mentioned in an earlier chapter, bringing the outlying districts under the administration of a now expanded city district has had the effect of doubling the school enrollment in all but the largest of the five communities in which we interviewed. The outcome has been not only the construction of new high schools and junior high schools but also a more elaborate school bus system, expenditures to upgrade facilities in rural elementary schools, and broadened curricula.

Interestingly, some persons in both the cities and the rural areas have opposed consolidation on the grounds that taxes will increase—city people believing that "all those new buildings" are necessary only because of the influx of farmers' children, and rural people believing that now they will have to pay for fancier education than they really want. The truth of the matter is difficult to discover because of other changes affecting the tax base, but whatever the truth regarding its direct impact on taxes, consolidation has met heavy opposition in every town, enough to cause three special ballotings in one instance and to leave hard feelings in all instances.

Almost without exception, therefore, school board members, business leaders, clergymen, and teachers joined the superintendents in reporting to us that, "of all educational issues which have involved people in your community in recent years," consolidation of the school district has been paramount. And the real reason for most of the opposition —if superintendents' and board members' testimony is to be trusted—has had (in rural areas) less to do with taxes than with parochial pride, and (in cities) less to do with taxes per se than with a variety of personal interests.

Basketball is a religion, we were told. Especially in the rural areas, games played by the then local schools symbolized to hinterland people their own identity and their distinctiveness from townspeople. One rural man proudly claimed not to have missed a contest in thirty-five years, "even when I had shingles." As Coleman discovered in the high schools he researched, which varied in size and location, competitive interscholastic athletics is frequently the prime activity around which an entire community can unite.[4] And a rural community has even fewer alternatives in this regard than a town of 10,000. Take away its symbol of distinction, and many will be disturbed, perhaps especially those whose sons must now contend with a wider range of talent in order to make the team (we uncovered a few such instances), but to a lesser degree everybody else as well. Their disturbance, it should be clear, is not simply over basketball but over what a basketball team symbolizes. From the smallest town in our sample to the largest, rural opposition to consolidation seems to have stemmed chiefly from this kind of sentiment. We heard it from superintendents and board members, from city people and rural, from those who had favored consolidation and those who had opposed it. Basketball is a religion to these people, but it is an outward sign of an inward concern for their own rural way of life.

Perhaps that point will be clearer if we note other manifestations of rural opposition to consolidation. In one community, the superintendent began his formal campaign for enlarging the district by hosting his school bus drivers at a dinner. Explaining to them the advantages to "everyone" if the various schools were merged, he hoped that by evangelizing these couriers he could also convince the parents of the children they carried. This astute administrator is the one who also set up parallel bus schedules, one immediately after school, another two hours later, so that farmers' children can if they choose participate in extracurricular activities.

Some sort of negative confirmation comes from the one community of the five which is near enough in distance to a very large city that it is attracting suburban commuters. Opposition to consolidation in this community has come

4. James C. Coleman, *The Adolescent Society* (Glencoe, Ill.: The Free Press, 1961).

as expected from most of the surrounding area but not from that portion which is suburban rather than rural.

In general, then, rural opposition to consolidation has resulted from a desire not to "lose our school." But with the exception of only a few small areas still holding out, these five school districts have expanded and now contain most of their outlying territories. To some extent, capitulation has come because, by being unable or unwilling to plan for the school-age population explosion, a rural area with one school building simply could not contain all of its own pupils. But to a larger extent, capitulation resulted from a recognition by a majority of rural residents that better education would be available for their children. *Better* in this case means larger and more varied facilities, more qualified teachers, an expanded curriculum, in short, a more progressive school program.

**Opposition from Townspeople**
Paradoxically, what little opposition to consolidation per se that came from within the towns came for precisely the reason it was favored by those from without—it meant "progressive" education, with fancy laboratories, bigger gymnasiums, more teachers. For many townspeople, however, progressive education became objectionable only after its costs became apparent. As one school board member put it, "People in town here didn't oppose reorganization of the district—not until it came time to build new buildings."

This building stage is the one in which all five school districts now find themselves, and therefore the immediate political context for educational affairs in these Midway communities for the past few years is one of taxes—for new buildings, remodeling, teachers' salaries, and instructional innovations. In every town the superintendent moves as far in these directions as he can, frequently with powerful support but always with powerful opposition. As one Chamber of Commerce president described his town's superintendent to us, "If we let this guy go, he'd double our taxes for schools and build schools we don't really need."

But the tax issue narrowly conceived is not the whole of the historicopolitical context for educational affairs, even in the towns. In addition there are the problems of school location and Federal aid, of school board membership and personnel administration, of gymnasium size and swimming pool site. In one community, for instance, population growth in a hill section has been so enormous that it is the logical site for the new Junior High which everyone agrees needs to be built. But commerce still centers in the downtown area, and merchants fear that additional construction on the hill will mean loss of business to themselves. In several towns, as another instance, the possibility of using federal funds in the schools (for Headstart, remedial, or special education) has been opposed "in principle." Two communities are involved in the matter of whether to retain a system of appointed board members or shift to an election process, and several communities gave evidence of a nascent teachers' union or at least an organization of teachers willing to flex its muscles over salaries. In one of the five areas, public debate has raged over the seating capacity of the new high school gymnasium, and in another over whether a swimming pool should be part of the new high school or whether it should be built in a city park. These aspects of historico-political context, however, are only part of the environment of local decision-making; to understand the latter more fully, we must confront the realities of power in our five communities.

## The Context of Power at the Local Level

Perhaps because all five of the communities studied are relatively small and homogeneous in population, the basic outlines of power distribution within them are similar. Idiosyncratic features are identifiable, but none significantly affected behavior in regard to schoolhouse religion. We can therefore characterize the five communities jointly, recognizing that actual characteristics of power distribution and usage may be slightly variant in each. For these purposes, we use power as a summary term representing possession of those resources which make it possible to shape the policies and practices of the local educational system. We have traced the locus of power so defined through reconstructing actual decisional processes and through hypothetical and reputational inquiry seeking to identify the sources of cues and pressures. In each community, a set of men, groups, corporations, or other entities possess relatively more of these resources than do others, and this preponderance leads us to refer to them as power holders. Because the actions of these power holders are normally concerted after a process of internal bargaining and negotiation, it is realistic to refer to them as a single unit or power structure with respect to educational affairs.

Several different types of resources give rise to power in these communities. Economic resources are most significant, but these may take several possible forms. Perhaps the simplest and surest source of power is the possession of great wealth (by community standards). No large landholder, investor, or entrepeneur can extract himself from a power position within such a community unless he works very hard at the task. This is true, if for no other reason, because the major sources of wealth are by definition the major taxpayers of the community. As such, they hold the capacity to subvert the daily operation of schools and city government by refusal to pay, or by engaging in a time-consuming law-suit to contest assessments or rates in any given year. Characteristically, the leading taxpayers of any community, whether they be businesses or individuals, are consulted about tax levels and contemplated projects in advance of public announcement, and their consent is gained—perhaps in ex-change for reductions in the scale of the project or for assurances regarding future improvements. The potential re-location of a major employer, and the community's need for his support, leads to a level of deference which if any-thing is in excess of his actual capacity to force compliance with his preferences. The fewer the number of such major units of wealth, of course, the more significant each becomes, for there is less chance that they will be split into counter-vailing groups on any given issue. In one town, for example, a single utilities plant provides fully 60 percent of city and county taxes. That the school board regularly consults exec-utives of this plant before deciding on a new school building seems perfectly understandable, therefore.

Another type of economic resource is a central position within the community's business life. Even in the absence of great wealth, bankers, real estate brokers, and lawyers are in a position to facilitate the advancement of others (or, conversely, to handicap a person's pursuit of profit and advancement). In part, this position depends on the posses-sion of advance knowledge about investment opportunities or development plans, but it is also based on the capacity to provide crucial assistance to others at moments of need. Another kind of central position is that of dominant businesses; a department store, supermarket, theater, or newspaper can in various ways set marketing patterns for a community or establish priorities which other businessmen feel obliged to follow. The owners or managers of such enterprises frequently can assert the right to be consulted about local projects in advance of public announcement, and to reshape those that they perceive as in some way threatening. In some cases, economic necessities force businessmen to become engaged in local politics. We have just seen that in one community the downtown merchants are concerned about a projected Junior High which may be built "on the hill." It seems clear why a retailer can rarely afford to be indifferent to zoning arrangements, parking regulations, the level of police traffic enforcement, or tax demands; the very nature of his livelihood inserts him into the quest for power and the pursuit of the resources requisite to effective defense of his own interests. A situation is thus created where possessors of shares in the economic life of the community have both special reasons to be regular, long-term participants in local power relationships and also the resources to take part in such a process. In addition, most such political actors share in the prospect that business (and profits) will improve if only they can boost their communities to attract new business and new population; the hope of gain thus acts as an additional spur to involvement and cooperation.

Economic resources are not the only routes to power, nor are they sufficient even where they exist. Social status may give rise to the opportunity to hold power, as in the case of local doctors and other professional men. The special skills of doctors, dentists, lawyers, engineers, and others contribute to their social position and their resultant opportunities. Similarly, tradition may give rise to power, as in the case of long-established families in a community of low turnover. The habit of decades is hard to break, even where the current holder of the family name is not particularly anxious to be a mover and shaper of the community. In some cases institutional position (public office, minister of a leading church, or a position of leadership in a voluntary association) may offer an individual the platform from which to generate influence. We observed instances of all of these forms of power.

In all of the cases, however, with the possible exception of the holders of great wealth, a screen exists between the opportunity or resources which may lead to power and the actual possession of a share in the decision-making process. This screen is tacitly (and perhaps on occasion unconsciously) imposed by one generation of power holders upon the next, and it consists of some crucial standards and criteria of admission into the circle of acceptance as a power holder and participant in the community's decisional processes. A candidate must be a "regular guy"—one who is open, friendly, reasonably gregarious, and generally orthodox in goals and life style; he must be possessed of an apparently genuine concern for the success of the joint enterprise in which all are after all engaged, that is, he must have some sense of community spirit and boosterism, not just self-interest; and he must be adapted to a consensus style of operation in which extended negotiation succeeds in "feeling out" potential objections and satisfying them before action is formally proposed. Possessors of economic or other resources who are not strongly motivated and who do not conform to these criteria are not likely to enter the circle of those who share real decision-making capacity in any of our communities. Some men might try for years to enter the power structure and be unsuccessful; new residents could on the other hand move into such a group in short order if they demonstrated the right combination of qualifications.

In each of the communities investigated (and it must be remembered that they range only from small town to small city), we observed therefore a relatively small group of men with the motivation, recognized capacity, and entitlement to make at least preliminary judgments on most questions of scholastic importance. They see each other often enough—at Rotary, Kiwanis, church, country club, or private affairs—to be able to anticipate each others' reactions and to know the points at which group consensus would be ruptured. They do not themselves staff all of the governing bodies in the community, for that would be both unnecessary and provocative. Instead, they have representatives—nominees, aspirants, members, agents, or others who identify with their priorities and interests—actually on such bodies. Thus, school boards, along with city councils, draft boards, park and fire commissions, church vestries, etc., are linked loosely to the power structure and are normally guided by its sense of priorities and community spirit. Many of the members of such entities are perhaps unknowingly engaged in a process by which they are being trained and socialized into the proper priorities and skills which will lead to full-fledged membership in the power structure. No clear-cut hierarchy or command relationship exists, for none is necessary; but experienced members of such governing bodies know that they operate within a set of boundaries—and that their autonomy is dependent upon observing those boundaries and procedures. Such knowledge is as true of a small farmer who sits on the school board as it is of the third generation doctor who chairs the meeting. Consultation prior to any action is one prerequisite: "checking out" of the acceptability of any departure from established practices is so much a part of normal operating procedure that it raises no intimation of subservience. This tacit arrangement is one which enables smooth functioning of a variety of governing bodies even under circumstances where several members are "outsiders." Together with a congenial quiescence on the part of the general public, such agreement insulates responsible authorities against maverick "do-gooders" and Birch Society members alike. And it is so much a part of the fabric of local community life in each of our five communities that users of the term *power structure* feel obliged to smile apologetically at the triteness of their characterization. Not surprisingly, the school board meetings in each of these towns are open to the public (though visitors seldom show up); but also not surprisingly, the real business of the meeting has been conducted earlier—in nonpublic sessions.

### Local Elites: Principles of Action
The existence of such a narrow distribution of power in these communities carries crucial significance for the process of local response to Supreme Court policies. These local elites are the sources of cues to the general public, and their decisions as to what shall be done are likely to be completely controlling over local public policy. They are in many respects independent, or at least subject only to their own locally-generated priorities and preferences. We

must therefore explore first their general principles of action, and then the nature of their responses to the prayer decisions.

Perhaps the paramount principle of operation of the local power structure examined here is that of conflict-avoidance. Nothing is perceived as so inappropriate, threatening, and undesirable as open conflict between key members of the community over questions of local public policy. On occasion, conflict between the establishment and segments of out-groups may be unavoidable and even necessary; but failure at conciliation or of obedience to local norms resulting in conflict within the establishment would be tantamount to a breakdown of the community's social fabric.

There are good reasons behind this paramount commitment to conflict-avoidance, many of which also maximize the chances that conflict *will* be avoided. For one thing, members of the power structure are in constant contact with each other for reasons of business, pleasure, and social obligation. Out of sheer interpersonal necessity, they cannot afford personal bitterness or animosity. They also have multiple goals in mind: none of them is so committed to single causes that he can afford to alienate others if that is what it would take to get his way. Instead, they all know that they will be dealing with each other in regard to different issues for the foreseeable future, and today's loss to a temporary antagonist may be more than made up for by to-morrow's opportunity for an alliance with the very same person. Further, it is cheaper and more efficient to reach accommodations among essentially like-minded men, even if one price of such a process is securing less than complete satisfaction for one's goals. Besides, there is great effort involved in carrying a controversy out into the public cognizance—perhaps far more than the goals involved are worth. And possibly most limiting of all, involvement of the general public renders the outcome unpredictable; indeed, it is even possible that the outcome might be a diminution of the power position of the entire power structure, a possibility that no sensible member would want to promote. For all these reasons, therefore, open and visible conflict is carefully avoided. If an issue were such that conflict seemed for some reason totally unavoidable, the issue or problem itself would probably be deferred or defined away by general agreement in order to avoid disruptive effects.

A second general operating principle of these power structures is their adherence to an ethic of low taxation and low expenditure within the community. Because they are predominantly made up of businessmen and others whose interests are chiefly economic, they take a short-range, tradesman's viewpoint with regard to improvements whose beneficiaries are the general public or the community at large—such as schools, parks, hospitals, etc. Where the return to the business community is clearer, such as the development of parking facilities, access roads, or airports, a greater receptivity is found. Even in such areas, however, the general ethos would be apparent, if only because not all segments of the business community would benefit directly from any one improvement. The result of this low-tax, low-spend ethic is to erect barriers against any new investments in buildings or services, despite the fact that some such improvements might in the long run reduce total expenditures or effect economies of operation. Although construction of a new and larger school building might, for example, permit greater efficiency of operation and permit cheaper expansion in the future, it would be resisted in the present if existing facilities could by any adjustment be made to serve for the moment. The rationale for such action would be the dual one that money not spent today is money saved and that refusal to act on one perceived need postpones the day when public aspirations and expectations will inevitably move on to another goal which will also cost money. Build a new gymnasium for the high school this year, some businessmen complained, and next year there will be a campaign for a new swimming pool, and then probably for a summer recreation program to go with it.

But this is not to say that the power structures of these communities are entirely negative toward community development projects. Indeed, a third general operating principle which coexists (sometimes tenuously) with the low-tax, low-spend ethic is that of civic pride and boosterism. The more far-sighted members of the local power structures not only want to attract investment and new industry to their communities (primarily as a means of spreading the tax load) but also realize that adequate public services are a factor in such development. New businesses may be attracted principally by relatively low tax rates and assessments, but also they often seek a well-trained work force, adequate educational opportunities for the children of executive-level employees, and available recreational facilities—all of which normally require at least a minimum level of quality in the school system.

Not all civic pride and boosterism rests on such a crass foundation, of course. We have already noted that the success of the local high school's athletic teams is a matter of great importance in relatively isolated communities. But the school is a focus of citizen self-image and community spirit also because it provides one of the major routes of social mobility; it is the key to escape from the community for the children of those who remain caught in it. Each of the superintendents was quick to point out the proportion of his high-school students who went on to college. Much civic pride and sense of self-fulfillment is bound up in the school system, therefore, and local power structures respond to this fact.

What we have been describing so far is a loosely associated body of men who hold a preponderance of power within each of our five communities, and who act on certain generally shared principles in most matters. Those who share decision-making roles do so in part because of their possession of economic or social resources and in part because they have demonstrated the characteristics of attitude and behavior which qualify them for admission into the circles of influence. Because of their occupations and their locations within the community social structures, these men have access to information about forthcoming events, obligations, requirements, or issues long before the general public. Through intra-elite communication channels, negotiations take place between those most deeply affected by forthcoming matters, and an accommodation generally acceptable to all is worked out and inserted into the official arenas of decision-making. Thus, most issues have in effect been acted upon by the power structure before they even come to public notice. In some cases, of course, an issue or problem is projected into local discourse without warning. In such cases, official decision-makers can usually be trusted to know power structure preferences without having to ask for guidance, but the process of "checking out" will probably occur anyhow, if only to enable official decision-makers to demonstrate that they know how the game should be played.

Local power structures do not hold a monopoly on all available forms of power within their communities. From time to time, "outsiders" may mobilize popular outrage or aspirations in such a way as to force the power structures to modify their plans and practices; alert leaders may trim their sails in anticipation of such efforts, so that local establishments appear benevolent and public-interest oriented. For example, civil rights for black Americans is an issue which has impinged on several of these communities, bringing about a new teacher hiring policy in two instances and a summer teenage employment agency in another. Yet there is little evidence to suggest that local decision-makers personally desired such changes, that they were doing more than responding to "outside" pressures.

On occasion, particular issues or leadership may so arouse opposition that the outcome represents a defeat for the existing power structure. Thus, school district consolidation has had a stormy course in most of these towns, with delays brought about by dissident factions through the use of referenda. These defeats indicate that the applicable leaders were not doing their job very well, of course, but they are far from disastrous events. What sustains the power structures of these local communities and permits them to endure as the governing bodies is the fact that their members are in the game for the long run; by occupation, interest, skills, habit, social position, and economic capacity, power structure members will continue to influence outcomes—if not in regard to an election today, then as to the budget or other actions of officials tomorrow. In this way they may simply outlast and exhaust their opponents. Amateurs who wish to compete for influence with such an establishment, even in a small community, must either become professionals in the process of governance or suffer the consequences of eventually being ignored and isolated. In part this explains why ministers only rarely become full-fledged members of local power structures and why Birch Society flare-ups have been without effect. In neither case is there the staying power, time investment, or willingness to play the game that leads to real power.

Nor do established power structures normally feel the need to control all aspects of life, or even of official public practices, within their communities. It is enough to set and manage the general outlines of what is acceptable and ap-

propriate through occasional illustrative acts, symbolic ges-
tures, rewards, or punishments. A broad general consensus
on profit-seeking, community development, civic pride, personal advancement, and something like "the good life"—
all fairly basic elements of American political ideology—is
usually enough to structure behavior within acceptance limits,
and little explicit enforcement is necessary. Many details of
local policy are beneath the notice of power structures, or
tacitly entrusted to management by a few specially interested
persons. Major decisions, of course, such as plans to spend
millions of dollars on a new school, are proper subjects for
consultation. Even here, however, those who prepare such
plans are normally sufficiently sensitive to establishment preferences that they can anticipate reactions, adjust their plans,
and secure acquiescence with a minimum of controversy.
They would of course approach power structures with recognition that opposition might be fatal, so their plans would
be adaptable to the many vetos existing within the community.

Thus the environment for school policymaking is permissive rather than dictatorial. Many channels of communication
and liaison with power holders are available, and used, so
that the acts of the schools are taken either in the image
of power-structure preferences or within the bounds of con-
ferred discretion. At any time, of course, erroneous use of
discretion in a matter then or later conceived to be of importance could result in revocation of the grant of discretionary authority. Everything is contingent, but the capable school
officials we interviewed know the range of their discretionary
authority, and revocation has not been necessary.

**School Officials in the Local Power Context**
The role of the school superintendent and of the school
board is set by the character of power distribution and patterns or usage which we have just described. In a formal
sense, the superintendent is quite a free agent, able to act
as his conscience would have him do; in the practical world,
however, he must be finely tuned to basic local power-
structure preferences, and he must develop a high sensitivity
for determining who holds real power and who may be ignored with impunity. He does have an area of real discretionary authority, because he is after all the subject matter
expert who knows the standards and requirements of the
educational bureaucracy; he has an informational monopoly

on what is going on in the school system, and the school board knows only what he tells them; he sets the agenda and structures the issues for school board action; and not least in this day and age, he is highly mobile and sought after by other school systems. But life will be easier—both in terms of his personal relations with other power holders, some of whom are likely to be his personal friends and referents, and in terms of achieving his professional goals for the community's schools—if he consistently exercises that discretion in accordance with power-structure preferences, however inchoate these may be at times. Even if an action never comes to light, he will have the confidence that he cannot be embarrassed by revelations while he is in the midst of negotiations to secure some goal which he considers important and for which he needs power-structure support. The point is that school superintendents have reasons to conform all of their actions—including those of little contemporary significance which are within their discretionary spheres—to the perceived preferences of local power holders. To do otherwise would be to jeopardize chances to secure the goals that the superintendent considers essential for the school system.

It is this need to secure and maintain a position from which to obtain high-priority goals that keeps the school superintendent so sensitive to power-structure preferences. He must be able to anticipate what those preferences would be if a subject were to become important enough to generate preferences regarding it, and long in advance of the time when the matter might arise to such a level. His question is, "Could what I do here in regard to this detail today possibly embarrass or antagonize power-structure members at some future time or under some possible circumstances?" Clearly, this is not a situation which encourages boldness, yet every one of the superintendents we interviewed is, above all, sensitive to precisely this question. As one clue to this sensitivity, for example, we noted that each of the superintendents, in interviews, *volunteered* the term *power structure.* It was a term we never initiated in conversations with them, yet each apparently finds his world easier to understand if labeled that way.

A capable superintendent of course develops ways of intuiting reactions or shaping understanding so that he may proceed with both daily affairs and the obtaining of his long-range goals, and distinct styles of accommodation to relationship problems with the power structure are noticeable among our superintendents. All are superior politicians, in the best sense of that term: they serve as brokers among interests, providing representation for a variety of viewpoints and yet operating effectively to promote their own perceptions of community interests. But their styles vary sharply. One sees himself as the passive agent of the community and the school board; not surprisingly, he is a man who has been through several local controversies and suffered defeats and personal attacks as a consequence. In his late years, by the time of our study, he has drawn back into more of of a caretaker role. He initiates very little, and then only reluctantly. In such a role, he can hardly be criticized severely, nor would the power structure be likely to be embarrassed.

Another distinctive style is that of Superintendent F., who is naturally oriented toward athletics and associated boosterism and therefore finds it congenial to develop an image of the brash, energetic, bull-in-the-china-shop-but-loveable official. With this public image, resentment of specific acts will be blunted; people see Mr. F. as such a hearty fellow, so deeply committed to an unbeaten basketball record, that he could not intend harm by his action. Mr. F. can then do with impunity, or at least with assurance that he will not create difficulties for the power structure, things for which the previous superintendent might have suffered severely.

But the modal style, common to three of the five superintendents whom we studied, is that of careful and constant politico. Touching all bases, sounding every possible interested party, performing all the rites of social and political power-maximizing, these men have developed images of influence well in excess of their actual power. They constantly play the game of informing, consulting, and structuring public understanding so as to build support for themselves and their school projects. Writing news releases, calling in first bus drivers and then cafeteria workers to wine and dine them and gain their support for consolidation of schools, overinforming responsible board members with trivia to preclude criticism for lack of advance notice of an issue, acquiescing "in principle" with ministers' proposals and asking them to do the impossible by drawing up an agreed program—all of these techniques are the acts of prudent, sophisticated politicians. By working at their jobs full-time and overtime, these superintendents extract every bit of influence consistent with their vulnerability to the preferences of local power structures. All of these activities are undertaken, of course, for the purpose of being able to have the best chance to gain the goals that the superintendents think are most crucial to the future success of the schools. In effect, the superintendents bank good will, respect, images of influence, and other assets against the time when they have to expend some of this capital to achieve vital goals. And only for very important goals is it worth expending such capital; until then, they husband their resources.

### The Principles of Action in Operation

These are the circumstances of power and priority in which the Supreme Court's prayer decisions were announced. Amidst intricate local power relationships, juggling many long-term goals and half-completed projects, with responsibility for all the many facets of school operation, superintendents had to weigh the direction and intensity of their personal commitments to both prayers and the Court against the realities of power and preference in their environments. We have already seen that their personal attitudes are generally supportive of the Court's rulings, but the issue lacked salience and their commitment was low in intensity. A brief summary of contextual forces in this area shows that their lack of real concern for elimination of schoolhouse religion was almost inevitable; any significant step to comply formally with the Court's decisions would probably have cost them dearly in credits with existing power structures. We need to know how.

Men of power in these communities are not deeply committed to prayers in the schools. Indeed, their preference for religious observances is a marginal one at best. Newspaper editors uniformly insisted that opinion leaders strongly favored prayer and Bible reading in the schools, but this seems to us to overstate the extent of concern for this issue on the part of real power-holders (as opposed to prominent ministers and articulate individuals). What is absolutely paramount to all of the men of power, however, is that they not be embarrassed by having to take stands on difficult questions or by having conflict erupt in the community.

Superintendents and school board members could hardly be unaware of the priority attached to these principles in their respective power structures. Conflict is particularly to be avoided in those instances where numbers of people are likely to become involved. Such an eventuality not only renders the outcome quite unpredictable but also promotes public attention to a wide range of issues and creates levels of public engagement in politics which threaten continued power-structure control. The issue of schoolhouse religion, in the eyes of all school officials, held high potential for wide public involvement; as such, it was particularly important to existing power structures that conflict not be permitted to develop.

Further, there was a deep-seated inertia regarding teacher discretion in the matter of schoolhouse religion. The result was an array of prayers, Bible reading, and other religious activities in the schools. No changes could have been made in the long-established practices of teachers without the most formal and specific policy declaration and enforcement, with all the visibility and local outrage which that would imply. Many public school teachers also serve as Sunday school teachers, which suggests both the nature of their preferences and the extent of their opportunities to develop opposition to any change in school practices. This pattern of familiar practice, teacher support, and prospective opposition to efforts to change might have been sufficient by itself to discourage any official attempt to institute anything other than the most strongly sought policy.

Finally, it is clear that each superintendent had many priorities which far outranked schoolhouse religion. All of our superintendents faced consolidation, building, taxation, and other more important curriculum issues on which opposition could be anticipated and for which power-structure support would be necessary. Controversy in regard to religious observances could seriously endanger the delicate bases of support for these strongly sought goals; almost nothing was to be gained by acting to carry out the Supreme Court's rulings, but much might be irretrievably lost.

In these circumstances, our politician-superintendents produced a simple but inordinately appropriate response: they did nothing. Their power holders around them, with equal serenity, did nothing. And nothing happened in any of our five communities. *Nothing* was, after all, the perfect solution. Depending upon interpretation, doing nothing amounted to defiance of the Court, perpetuation of the status quo, compliance with American ideology (albeit with a tortuously narrow view of the Court's mandate), and transcendence of the whole problem. More importantly, it avoided conflict and preserved intact the entire supply of capital for the much more important goals yet to be sought. It was a brilliant if easily come upon solution.

The actions actually taken by the five superintendents conform to the single principle of exalting this response of doing nothing. Their behavior may be seen as a case study of the matter in which power structures act to depress conflict and manage acquiescence for their preferences within local communities. When queried, superintendents gave assurances to local newspapers and ministers alike that there would be no changes. When ministers sought to test whether the schools could still be the scene of religious observances, they were encouraged to come forward and perform. In the meantime, teachers could be relied upon to continue their traditional practices, thereby reassuring any interested parents or other extraschool inquirer. Activists groups with both pro and con positions—from the Birch Society to the Civil Liberties Union—were blandly ignored or brusquely deflected as part of the tacit strategy of avoiding conflict.

The crucial achievement engineered by our superintendents was the insulation of the local schools from the waves of reaction against the Court which were rolling through Midway. We have seen that school prayer was a lively issue for many people, but the focus was national and distant; the superintendents succeeded in preventing any link-up of this nationally oriented outrage with a local target. How adroitly they blocked such translation into a local controversy may be seen from one superintendent's deflection of the potential troublemaking of a strong right-wing group— for here was a sector of traditional antischool sentiment, violently opposed to the Supreme Court, and rabidly orthodox in religion. Yet the *Schempp* decision came, stirred up this group for a while, and left without touching the local schools at all.

### The Principle of Deflection

In the largest of the five Midway communities we investigated, there is an active right-wing contingent organized around the wife of a local clergyman. It contains fundamentalist Protestants, John Birch Society members, and others of the sort that David Riesman several years ago called the "curdled indignants." It also has access to a radio station which broadcasts a variety of religious and patriotic messages, reports news, and in general keeps quite visible (or at least audible) the activities of its supporters. In the past it has contended with the public schools, chiefly over presumed communist control of the curriculum and the nature of speakers who are and are not invited to speak at the high school assemblies.[5] The public schools, in other words, are viewed by this group as enemies, or at least in the control of enemies.

The school-prayers decisions, needless to say, did not go unnoticed by these people. In addition to their radio broadcasts, they campaigned in shopping centers, with the help of a "hillbilly band," to get signatures on a constitutional amendment petition. Much publicity was sought, much hoopla surrounded their efforts, and many names were recorded. But because the schools were already defined as enemies, already in this instance viewed as godless and assumed to be without religious observance, the right-wing group never bothered to focus on the local schools. The superintendent, by doing nothing and avoiding all public statements, escaped having his local schools brought into this arena of anti-Court sentiment. We interviewed one of the major figures in this right-wing group, reporting to him that yes indeed prayers and Bible reading persisted in the schools of his city. He could hardly believe it!

One will never know, of course, how different things might have been had the anti-Court sentiment been focused on the local situation. But it is worth at least the speculation that, had such localization occurred, lines would have been drawn, a description of the actual religious practices would have been made public, parents of school children would have been drawn into the fray, and finally, the superintendent would have been forced to act on schoolhouse religion. As it happened, he wasn't.

5. We were able to interview both the present superintendent and his retired predecessor, who still resides in the city. Both reported extensively on the history of the schools' relationship with the group in question.

## Other Factors Permitting Superintendents' Inertia

On some occasions, superintendents went beyond mere conflict-avoidance to make use of proreligious sentiment as a means of advancing their own strategic positions in the community. One superintendent, for example, deliberately went to the schools from time to time to take part in religious observances. Not only did this provide cues for his teachers, but it enabled him to build capital with various elements in his community. This cynical fence-mending (the superintendent personally favored the Court's ruling) was not typical, but it shows the extent to which a politically sensitive official with many higher-priority goals can go to serve the needs of powerful people in the social structure to which he is responsive.

These actions and avoidances of action by our superintendents were made possible, of course, by the absence of pressure from state-level officials. If there had been opinions, instructions or perhaps even public statements from relevant state officials, the issue would have been much more difficult to avoid. Parents, ministers, teachers, or others would probably have forced the superintendents to take some kind of stand, which would in turn have sparked further reactions and controversy. In the totally permissive situation in which they were obligingly left by state officials, however, the superintendents were free to serve local power-structure needs by doing nothing.

Superintendents uniformly defended their inaction by pointing to their many important priorities and emphasizing the need to conserve their political capital for such purposes. On one level this is entirely natural and understandable behavior. But at a deeper level of analysis, it implies that public officials can also serve unwittingly as effective agents on behalf of their local power structures. Husbanding their capital, adding to it by depressing conflict and avoiding issues, in their own eyes they were merely political realists. But one might ask whether *any* issue, including their high-priority goals, would ever be sufficiently important in their eyes to warrant the expenditure of their long-amassed political credits. Indeed, they may even suspect that any effort to employ their stored resources for purposes opposed by power holders would reveal that their capital is in fact non-existent. What this can mean, of course, is that many appar-

ently well-meaning people actually promote power-structure
preferences and policies to which they are opposed, all in
the name of achieving some greater priority in the future—
only to find that the critical moment never comes, or the
"capital" so carefully stored is illusory and ineffective.

And what of the citizen who might happen to feel that
the law of the land should be obeyed? The principles of
power and behavior examined in this section show that he
would be ignored, dismissed as irrelevant or dangerous, or
viewed as a social misfit. Public officials and the local power
structures to whose needs they are responsive had many
reasons for continued noncompliance with constitutional requirements as articulated by the nation's highest Court. Not
in quite such blunt language, of course: most individuals,
including power-structure members, asserted their willingness
and desire to obey the law of the land. But they just had
other needs and goals right at the moment, and so they
went on about their real business as they perceive it—the
business of self-preservation and power-maximizing. For nonelites, the situation might be frustrating.

**The Impotence of Nonelites**
Opinion polls confirm common sense on at least one point:
people can always be found on both sides of any issue. We
are not surprised to find in every region of the country,
therefore, at least some who applauded the Supreme Court's
1962 and 1963 decisions. It is as inconceivable that everyone
favored schoolhouse religion as it is that everyone favored
the Court's outlawing schoolhouse religion. And the ordinary
belief is probably that even the "little man," armed with the
knowledge that the highest court in the land upholds his
viewpoint, can find a way to make his sentiments known.
With federal law behind it, even the smallest minority
should be emboldened to speak out, to investigate—in this
instance, to demand compliance.

It is therefore reasonable to believe that even in the smallest of these Midway communities, at least a few persons
who wanted school prayers eliminated might have been
listened to. And yet, though a voice or two might have been
raised, we uncovered no evidence to suggest anyone was
listening. The little man was clearly impotent on the matter
of school prayers.

Who are logical candidates for this role of dissident troublemaker? In Midway, Roman Catholics could have been. The Midway schools we investigated were more or less acknowledged Protestant parochial, and the King James Version was the Bible read almost exclusively. Should not some Catholic priest or layman have taken advantage of the 1963 ruling to challenge this offensive practice? Up to 10 percent of the populations of these towns are Catholic, and there is a Roman Catholic church in each. Yet no Catholic protest against "establishment" of Protestantism in the public schools occurred.

Jews, of course, represent another minority who might have objected to the establishment of Christianity in public schools. In four of the five communities there are one or two Jewish families; in the fifth, enough Jews to support a part-time, circuit-riding rabbi. Jehovah's Witnesses constitute another group which has traditionally objected to school religious practices, as have Seventh Day Adventists. These groups are also represented in the five Midway towns, and yet, as in the case with Roman Catholics, none of them challenged the religious status quo in the schools.

It is appropriate now to pursue the question of the inertia of those local persons who might have tried to bring about change. In a general way, we shall see how impotent are the nonelites in places like these Midwest communities. But since such a statement comes close to saying that the powerless are without power, we must elaborate on it by noting three ways in which this impotence is manifested.

First, a number of potential challengers are impotent because they lack power to reward the school system for complying with their requests or to punish it for failing to do so. Thus, even on the occasions when their voices are heard, these people may be summarily dismissed by school administrators as trivial annoyances. For example, one principal with whom we talked received a complaint from a Jehovah's Witnesses parent over her child's obligatory flag saluting. The teacher's response was to have the child *hold* the flag while his classmates saluted, a solution the principal called "brilliant," but hardly reflective on his or the teacher's part of a genuine appreciation of a minority position. We do not know how the mother in this case felt about the solution.

One superintendent told us of the large number of fundamentalist Protestant churches in his town. Their ministers and members are, however, "uneducated and totally irrelevant to the aims of the schools." In another town, where the superintendent claimed to know not only the present school board members but also everyone who might ever be elected to the board, a fundamentalist clergyman ran for the board on a platform of cleaning the school libraries of dirty books. He got very few votes, it is true, but the disdain with which the superintendent discussed his case with us reflects some of the reasons why.

We have no interest—in this discussion—in the substantive merits of these cases. Certainly an argument can be made why administrators must, if they are to govern at all, protect themselves from every whim and minority sentiment among their constituents. But it is the fact of that protection, not its merits, that we point to here. Thus, virtually all issues confronting the school boards in these Midway communities are decided informally, over private lunches for example, and only then are they brought up and presented unanimously at public meetings, to which hardly anyone comes. We are not arguing that another procedure would bring about more effective school administration but only that with this procedure and others like it, the little voices are even less likely to be listened to. One reason why no little voices challenged the schoolhouse religion practices, therefore, may be that if and when they did, nobody would be attuned to hear.

Another reason for the impotence of nonelites on this issue, however, lies in their willingness to live with what they perceive to be majority wishes. The rabbi in the one town with enough Jews to support a synagogue was quoted in the local newspaper shortly after the *Schempp* decision as saying that in his view the Supreme Court had not made illegal the schools' use of the Lord's Prayer. Since it most patently had, one finds a reasonable explanation of the rabbi's behavior not in his inadequate legal understanding but in his all too human desire to protect his flock from the ire of the Christian majority. Each of the superintendents and their school systems, after all, are careful to take *some* pains to protect religious minority interests; the rabbi may very likely have calculated that here was one point he was willing to concede in return for others already won or yet to be fought.

Similarly, the Catholic priests with whom we talked could not get excited over Protestant prayers and a Protestant Bible in the public schools. For several of them the use of public school bus transportation by parochial school pupils —an economic issue, it might be noted—was a very real matter, and one on which they spoke out and were listened to. But, except for one who saw in the Court's decisions simply additional evidence of America's secularization, no priest seemed much concerned that his parishioners were being hurt by the public schoolhouse religion in his community.

This acquiescence on the part of some who might be expected to express concern, is, we think, related to our earlier discussion of the "schoolman mentality." There is a sense in which professional educators are alert to religious minority interests, and that is in regard to coercion. If Jews and Catholics, Jehovah's Witnesses and Unitarians, do not *feel* forced to engage in particular religious practices, then when the Supreme Court renders a judgment outlawing a practice on the grounds that it is implicitly coercive, not surprisingly these minorities may be quite unconcerned to test the question.

We have been using the terms *nonelites, powerless, little man,* and *religious minority* more or less synonymously. Obviously this can be misleading, and we need to clarify the matter before making the third and final point. Earlier in this chapter we saw that persons in positions of power in school affairs really did not get concerned over school prayers. Their concerns lay elsewhere. By *nonelites* or those other labels, therefore, we mean those persons who, on this issue, might have been concerned. Quite clearly, then, the nonelite will be different on different issues, even though those who constitute the elite in school affairs may remain fairly constant.

With this clarification in mind we can now suggest a third reason why the nonelites concerned about school prayers failed to challenge religious practices in public schools. That reason has to do with the fact that school prayers constitute above all a style issue, not an economic interest issue. Indeed, it is probably a style issue par excellence since it is almost impossible to see how anybody stands to win or lose a cent on it. But because school prayers constitute a style issue, there is little available structure through which the issue can be approached. This is not the case with all style issues, of course, and neither is it the case in some regions with school prayers. In the Bible Belt, for example, or in areas with sizeable concentrations of non-Christians or non-Protestants, organization and interest groups ready to channel religiopolitical sentiments may abound. But in Midway no such organizations exist at the community level, and, in an earlier chapter, we saw how the relevant state-level organizations backed off from the fray—for reasons which many might regard as perfectly understandable.

Consider the difficulty in these small communities, therefore, which the few dissidents will have in acting on their desire to change the religious practices in their public school. Not only will they have trouble activating any of the established nuclei of power, but they will probably have trouble even interesting anybody. Probably for this reason alone, then, the inevitable (if occasional) dissenters find a number of barriers in their way, even of bringing a law suit to have matters changed. They must be prepared to suffer not only the ill will of those who disagree with them but also the ill will of those in the power structure who see them as upsetting an already "resolved" issue. They must find the sympathy, or at least the help, of an attorney, witnesses, and maybe investigators. They must be willing to seek the financial backing for their effort. And they must be committed, of course, to the appropriateness of their actions.

Something of the strategic importance of available channels for making dissent felt is well conveyed in Vashti McCollum's account of her lawsuit which eventually outlawed religious instruction on school property—the 1948 *Illinois ex rel. McCollum* v. *Board of Education*. Her third chapter, significantly entitled "I Reach a Decision," describes her efforts to have her son relieved both of religious instruction and of discriminatory treatment in its place. Finding no success with teacher or school superintendent, she remembered the local Unitarian minister in her town of Champaign, Illinois. She contacted him, and he wrote on her behalf to the Chicago Action Council, who, by immediate return mail, wrote, "Tell that woman to go ahead. We will hire her attorney and pay all the legal bills." It was this group,

jointly with the Chicago Civil Liberties Union, that supported
Mrs. McCollum throughout her three-year legal battle.[6]

Of course, the McCollum case is not directly comparable.
She was initiating an *issue,* not simply asking the courts to
extend a ruling to cover another instance. Nevertheless, as
Mrs. McCollum recounts her experience, the ready availability of a supportive clergyman, and through him access
to money and lawyers, played a huge part in her willingness
to pursue her constitutional rights.

More subtle than the need for money and legal assistance,
however, is the fact that without available community structures for channeling their dissent, persons may not even
realize they do dissent. As we have observed elsewhere,[7]
public attitudes toward the Supreme Court generally are very
loosely organized and tend, to some extent in relation to
people's evaluation of the presidency, to be structured along
political party lines.

Something of this sort appears to have happened on the
particular issue of prayer and Bible reading when it was
handed down by the Court. Of course, attitudes formed in
response; we are not arguing they did not. And attitudes
formed to some degree along predictable lines, some of which
are reviewed in chapter 2 above. But one of the striking
features of attitude formation on the school-prayers issue is
the degree to which it, like many style issues, failed to follow
ordinary social structural lines. For example, one study, using
Minnesota Poll data from 1964, found that eight different
structural characteristics (including amount of formal education, religious affiliation, age, sex, and socioeconomic status)
could account for 20 percent of the variance among people's
1960 presidential vote. But on the question of whether
people favored or disfavored amending the Constitution to
allow for school prayers, these same eight characteristics
accounted for only 1 percent of the variance.[8]

These Minnesota data tell in a different way the same
story we related earlier in this chapter about the right-wing
group's success in collecting signatures for a Constitutional
amendment but its failure thereby to stir up controversy

6. Vashti Cromwell McCollum, *One Woman's Fight* (Garden City,
N.Y.: Doubleday, 1951). The quotation is from p. 29.

7. Dolbeare and Hammond, "The Political Party Basis of Attitudes,"
pp. 16–30.

8. Shettle, "An Analyses of Public Opinion."

over local school religion practices. Individuals might be quite concerned about the issue and with considerable fervor sign or not sign the petition. But without channels to relate sentiment on this issue to the structure of already existing local sentiments, their fervor is likely to dissipate before effecting any local changes. The historicopolitical context for school affairs, in other words, sets limits on the nature of the political issues which will qualify for admission into the arena of effective controversy. The schoolhouse religion issue, in the five Midway towns we investigated at least, just did not qualify.[9]

This situation is easy to understand when, as seen above, consolidation, taxes, and building schools make up the dominant context for any educational issue. And when those persons and groups who do have power in the educational arena will not hook on to a style issue like school prayers, that issue is doomed for neglect. It is not, then, simply a matter of nobody's listening to the nonelites who may be upset by school religious practices. Listening—or, more approriately, hearing—is a function not only of individuals' personal predispositions but also of the larger political context in which the hearing must take place.

**Schoolhouse Religion as a Style Issue**
But even style issues may get caught up in the political whirl of a community. The fact that schoolhouse religion did not is related also to its being a style issue of a religious nature. Up to now we have been concerned with the style nature of the issue since we wanted to indicate the relative absence of structured channels for the formation of opinion and the manifestation of dissent. As a style issue, we said, schoolhouse religion is less likely to enter the established political arena with clearly drawn sides, organized combatants, and so forth. Now, however, we want to emphasize

9. As these pages were written, the *New York Times,* 26 March 1969, contained a front-page story of several small towns in Pennsylvania in which schoolhouse religion had become a dominant political issue, and prayer and Bible reading had been resumed in their schools. In one of these towns, the group pressing for resumption was led by a lawyer "who was a Presidential supporter of George C. Wallace . . . [and] president of the Fayette County Anti-Tax Protest Committee." The reporter noted that "the school board was apparently in no mood to invite the wrath of that rapidly growing and militant group." In our view, the merger of the school-prayers group with an existing tax-protest group is significant.

not the style but the religious nature of the schoolhouse religion issue. Since the Supreme Court decisions we have been discussing deal specifically with religion, several more reasons for inertia can be identified.

The first of these has been touched on in chapter 5 where we discussed schoolmen and the American political culture. The free exercise of religion, we said then, is built into the educator's set of commitments—his mentality, we called it—far more than is the nonestablishment of religion. But if this is the case with professional educators, it is probably also true in some significant measure with Americans generally. The number of Americans who immigrated because of religious persecution provides a historical context for this phenomenon, of course, but more than this, there probably is a sense in which most citizens of the United States really do believe that everyone has a right to his own religious opinions. Religious persecution qua *religious* persecution has been rare in America; contrarily, most religious denominations and certainly the public schools have exalted the presence of religious diversity. Such a statement must be qualified in one important respect, as we shall see presently, but for now we want to make the general point: Americans believe in the legitimacy of multiple faiths.[10]

We might go even further: The legitimacy given religious pluralism in America represents a central tenet in what could be called the American creed. Certainly religious pluralism implies disagreement over those statements generally labeled creeds; yet, as many have observed, there is an identifiable—if vague—ethic or civil religion running through the interpretations of these religious creeds. Americans may differ on the latter, but to this common code they are supposedly committed.[11] This America creed, this "reli-

10. This point, of course, is one of the theses convincingly argued in Will Herberg, *Protestant, Catholic, Jew* (Garden City, N.Y.: Doubleday, 1955).

11. In this matter, Tocqueville might again be credited with seeing early what became commonplace observation a century later. See Alexis de Tocqueville, *Democracy in America* (New York: Vintage, 1954). Other important discussions include Walter Lippmann, *A Preface to Morals* (New York: Macmillan, 1929); Max Lerner, "The Constitution and the Court as Symbols," *Yale Law Review* 46 (1937) 1290–1319; Herberg, *Protestant, Catholic, Jew;* Robert N. Bellah, "America's Civil Religion," *Daedelus* (Winter 1967); and the papers comprising chap. 9 of Phillip E. Hammond and Benton Johnson, eds., *American Mosaic: Social Patterns of Religion in the U.S.* (New York: Random House, 1970).

gion of democracy," exalts differences and urges resolution of competing interests through peaceful means. It sets the stage for competition but it does not specify the goals for which competitors should strive. It acknowledges certain inalienable rights, but it also accents that what is "right" in any particular case is what the majority wants.

It is this last article of the American faith which we must consider here, for, though there is no denying the failure of most Americans to behave in perfect accord with their creed, neither is there any doubt that the existence of that creed influences their behavior. And the influence is seen in several ways. First of course is the transposing phenomenon we have just reviewed. After all, if one aspect of the Bill of Rights is mentally substituted for another, the person doing the substituting is unlikely to regard himself as unconstitutional or evil. Far from being a mistake owing to ignorance, then, this transposition could occur because it was buttressed by the American creed itself: "If school prayers remain, it is because the great majority want them *and minority rights are protected.*" "Who could possibly believe it morally correct to outlaw school prayer when no one here has ever objected?" "The federal government has no more right to force us not to pray than we do to force someone *to* pray." Such thoughts reflect not an active, contradictory expression of sentiment but a disbelief that current schoolhouse religious practices could be contrary to the American creed as embodied in the United States Constitution.

One consequence, therefore, is that if noncompliance in this case is a sin, it is a sin conducted with a clear conscience. The superintendents at least, and probably some other officials as well in these local school districts, know in some sense that their religious practices are illegal. But to them that illegality, if they were to think about it, serves a higher, more moral aim and thus causes little ethical problem. The American creed, in other words, not only prompts school officials to respect religious minorities' rights to "free exercise" but also justifies those school officials in their disregard of a "no establishment" ruling. Ideology, to put it still another way, activates behavior in the first instance but inhibits behavior in the second instance; ideology both initiates change and justifies the status quo ante.

We are hardly the first to point out how conveniently creeds or ideologies can justify the status quo. Indeed for some, that function forms the definition of ideology. But as many others have also pointed out, ideologies are not infinitely malleable. At some point persons have no choice but to forsake their creed or their self-interest; but short of this point, persons will find pursuit of self-interest more or less comfortable, depending upon how it squares with their creed. What we are saying in the present instance is that school officials were very comfortable retaining their pre–1962 religious practices because, though to do so might mean contradicting the Supreme Court, it also meant conforming with a vital part of the American creed underlying that Court—the part respecting religious differences and exalting majority rule.

The American creed not only led superintendents to transpose a no establishment meaning into a free exercise meaning, however. That creed places a high premium on religious peace, and thus it fostered noncompliance in another way by motivating school officials to avoid conflict over school prayers. The value placed on religious peace is manifest in several ways. Ministers, priests, and rabbis are given equal positions on the platforms of public ceremonies, but in return they are expected to make no exclusive claims, to glorify no particular differences, to content themselves with the lowest common religious denominator. Public officials (including school superintendents) are supposed to be religious, but they are not to make their particular religiousness a defining characteristic. Thus, in a paradoxical way noted by foreign observers since at least early in the nineteenth century, Americans seem to hold simultaneously the view that religion is exceedingly important in a man's character and the view that it does not matter much *how* a man is religious. We can safely ignore religious differences, the American creed seems to say, but look out that the differences don't lead to religious war!

It is in such a paradoxical context, then, that religious conflict seems to be regarded as a particularly heinous kind of conflict and is to be avoided at all costs. Other style issues (sex education, for example) might breach the solid community support for public schools, but presumably it can be contained or fought without jeopardizing the delicately

balanced American creed. Schoolhouse religion, we are suggesting, cannot; and therefore educational leaders are espe-
cialy loath to act in any way which might bring on such
an eruption.

But American creedal considerations apart, there is a second, uniquely religious, factor inhibiting compliance. Inas-
much as it appears to contradict the first factor, it therefore
stands as a qualification of it. The fact is that a significant
proportion of church-state legal issues which have impinged
on public education in the United States have been brought
up by fringe groups, as Tussman points out:[12] Jehovah's
Witnesses, Seventh Day Adventists, Freethinkers, and so
forth. In small communities at least, such as those we have
studied here, members of fringe groups are easily dismissed.
We have already noted that superintendents, though committed to religious pluralism, could safely ignore the few
offbeat religious families in their districts, taking care only
to acknowledge them but not feeling compelled to comply
with their requests. We want now to suggest further that
the precedent of fringe-initiated complaints over church-state
issues might well have the effect of inhibiting complaints by
persons who do not regard themselves as on the religious
fringe. Anyone who starts proceedings to have changes made
in the style with which a community acts puts himself auto-
matically in a minority position. But such a position is less
uncomfortable for some than it is for others. To be on the
religious fringe is to have the experience and necessary commitment needed for sustaining the certain discomfort to follow. But that historic connection probably means that persons
in the religious mainstream, regardless of how they feel
personally about the legal issue, are more likely to hesitate
before taking a public stand against the majority. We talked,
for example, to many "mainline" clergy in the five communities and found a number who were at least ambivalent about
the Court's 1962 and 1963 decisions, willing to grant legitimacy to the Court's reasoning. Not a one had raised a finger
to ensure compliance, however; perhaps the desire to avoid
making common cause with religious fringe groups is part
of the reason.

With the mention of clergy comes a third reason why,
because the issue is a religious issue, compliance has been

12. Joseph Tussman, *The Supreme Court on Church and State* (New
York: Oxford University Press, 1962).

less likely. As a religious issue, school prayers and Bible reading have had natural leaders—clergymen—readily available to help form opinion and argue for and against the Supreme Court's decisions. But clergymen, as we asserted earlier, are not typically part of a community's power structure, not usually power oriented, and, moreover, they have pressures on them not to be. If there is one reasonably well-documented fact in the sociology of church organization, it is that clergy are discouraged by the constraints of their position from entering the arena of politics.[13] To the degree a minister must play the shepherd-counselor role—as he doubtlessly must in smaller communities—then he is certainly constrained. And his mobility aspirations and experience may constrain him even further. Clergy in small towns are disproportionately drawn from young persons on the way up or older persons who are resigned to not moving up. Neither category produces a high degree of boldness. Thus it is that those persons most naturally equipped to galvanize and lead religious issues in the political arena are least likely to do so. In the context of small towns or nonmetropolitan states, if clergy don't lead religious issues, few others are ready to substitute.

### The Local Community as a Context for Inertia

We have discussed a number of features of local communities which are likely to render them inactive when it comes to carrying out federal policy directives. Given a historico-political context which is largely focused on school consolidation, taxes, and buildings; given a power structure which exalts unruffled community relations and school officials who have higher priority goals than altering school religious practices; given devices for ignoring complaints when they arise from the nonelite sector; and given the religious nature of the issue in question, it is no wonder that little occurred. These Midway communities not only failed to comply with Supreme Court rulings; they failed even to respond.

13. A number of studies could be cited at this point. An excellent one is Ernest Q. Campbell and Thomas F. Pettigrew, *Christians in Racial Crisis* (Washington, D.C.: Public Affairs Press, 1959), an investigation of Little Rock ministers' response to the school integration crisis in their city. A general discussion of clergy and politics is contained in N. J. Demerath III and Phillip E. Hammond, *Religion in Social Context* (New York: Random House, 1969), chap. 6.

# Part Three    Some Conclusions

# 7  National Policies
## and Local Consequences

We have begun to develop explanations for the frequently
observed fact that there is no necessary and direct relationship between a Supreme Court decision (or, perhaps,
other national enactments as well) and actual local practice. The tangible consequences of national efforts at
change, we have seen, are the product of an extended process involving many forces and people. The process only
starts with enunciation of a new national policy; groups,
corporations, individuals, and public officials then interact
as their priorities and power permit, shaping the eventual
outcome as nearly as possible to their preferred image.
Not all policies are equally pliable in their hands, of course.
Sometimes circumstances enable interested parties to affect
outcomes drastically; sometimes only marginally.

We shall now try to integrate our findings with two closely
related lines of research, judicial impact studies and
community power studies, in order to develop a more comprehensive interpretation of when, how, and under what
circumstances local factors shape ultimate response to
Supreme Court decisions. Subsequently we shall speculate

about what this pattern may mean in regard to the consequences of other national policies and for the process of nationally induced change generally.

## Determinants of the Outcome of Judicial Decisions
### A General View

Many factors bearing on eventual outcome are self-evident. Some were noted in chapter 1, and others have been noted in previous studies. What is not so obvious is the relationship and process of interaction among such factors that lead to varying responses in different contexts. At the risk of appearing to proliferate typologies, we shall offer a set of four categories of factors which, based on our findings, appear to shape response to Supreme Court rulings. Neither our findings nor those of previous research permit us to go further. Indeed, we shall argue at the close of this chapter that there is little utility in attempting to do so, but there is great utility in analyzing the political *processes* which determine whether or not local practices will actually change to conform to new national standards.

Of the four categories of factors shaping response to Court rulings implicit in our findings, the first two are *structural* in character, in the sense of being givens or properties of a situation which are constant for all settings: for example, objective components of the policy (decision) itself, or pre-existing characteristics of institutions and procedures. The next two are *behavioral* in character, varying between settings and people: for example, the attitudes and actions of leaders and publics in the context of distinctive ongoing state and local political processes. In some respects we shall be restating matters discussed elsewhere in this book, but this is the point at which all can be brought together. Although the analysis which follows draws specifically on our findings here regarding the consequences of a new church-state policy enunciated by the Supreme Court, we speculate that similar or analogous categories apply to other types of policies generated by other institutions of the national government.

### The Substance of the Decision

Self-evidently, response is affected by the nature of the decision or policy involved. The allocation of a benefit is more likely to engender cooperative action among recipients than is the imposition of a burden; a clear mandate for specific action more than an ambiguous or confusing one; an incremental change more than a drastic reorganization of established relationships; and so on. Perhaps less obviously, *who* is required to act may be just as important as *what* they are to do. Where prominent public officials carry clear responsibility for enforcement or other implementation, discretion is most confined and cooperation is most likely. Public officials of less prominence may enjoy somewhat more discretion over their behavior, although they too are subject to the role responsibilities inherent in their offices and to the availability of legal maneuvers forcing them to act in some fashion. If the policy requires behavioral change on the part of large segments of the general public, however, cooperation will be more dependent upon popular preferences, the nature of the inducements to conform to a new standard, and the relationship between the new policy and the established patterns of behavior in this area.

Each of these propositions is illustrated by our findings. The change called for was substantial, the mandate was somewhat ambiguous, and people were being asked to give up something they were in the habit of enjoying. There was no unavoidable obligation for prominent public officials to act, local officials had discretionary capacity to avoid implementing action, and there were no inducements for the general public to change its behavior from long-established practices. The characteristics of this decision, in other words, gave especially broad scope and opportunity to the shaping capacity of participants in the post–policy-making process.

*Institutional Mechanism and Procedures*

The existence of a bureaucracy with the primary function of implementing policies establishes one pattern of relevant forces and raises the prospects of conformity with the policy. A bureaucracy has the capacity to reach out, investigate, and persuade or coerce the objects of the policy into appropriate behavior. What is most likely to limit the power of indigenous forces to shape consequences, and therefore most likely to induce conformity, is a federal bureaucracy (such as the Social Security or Veterans Administration) and, after that, a state bureaucracy (such as welfare agencies). Less effective in this regard are multipurpose agencies without oversight capabilities, such as the courts. Courts must await the initiation of cases by parties with the psychic and financial capacity to challenge authoritative decision makers, and then they must act within narrow confines of the law and its application to the particular relationships of the contending parties. Further, courts' interpretations do not necessarily bind officials or others not actually before the court. Thus, the scope of court capability is very limited, rendering policies dependent on court-induced behavioral change highly responsive to local preference and discretion. In some circumstances, of course, officials must themselves resort to the courts in order to discharge their responsibilities, and then courts may be a more effective vehicle of structuring response to national policies. Where law enforcement officials are the objects of new policies, as in the case of the decisions clarifying defendants' rights, courts are in a relatively strong position to enforce compliance. This is because prosecutors must secure convictions of wrongdoers in order to do their jobs, and judges may simply dismiss cases if defendants' rights of counsel or freedom from police harassment have not been observed. Officials and investigators thus have little choice about conforming with constitutional interpretations in such areas. This assumes, of course, that they seek to discharge their responsibilities through the courts; in many cases, the impact of Supreme Court rulings may be diluted through informal administration of justice by law enforcement personnel.

The availability of institutional mechanisms and/or other established procedures is thus an important conditioning factor which structures the rewards and punishments influencing behavior in any particular area. In the case of school prayers, no institutional support was regularly available except the courts, and even their limited capabilities were contingent upon invocation by local people. With the prospect of no rewards and few punishments, local elements were especially free to exercise their own discretion.

*The Politicocultural Context*

The context of public attitudes and prior traditions and practices may vary sharply in different settings across the United States. We noted earlier the distinctive regional and state patterns of response to the school-prayer decision, and we examined evidence suggesting that these patterns were owing to the behavior of state officials and to varying public opinion toward both Court and prayers. Well-established traditions of state-level decision making on the one hand, or of strict laissez faire abdication to local discretion on the other, will each create their distinctive patterns of post–policy-making influences. Public attitudes toward the issue, as well as toward the Court as an institution, in other words, enter the equation. The legitimacy of the originating institution (in this case, the Supreme Court), if great in a particular context, will reduce the capacity of local forces to modify a policy initiative; correlatively, strongly held preferences (in this case, for prayer) will neutralize such feelings and restore initiative to local elites. In Midway, respect for the Court, we may safely assume, was not high, but preference was thought to be high for prayers, so local elites were free to act in accordance with their usual preferences.

The politicocultural context also becomes particularly important in determining whether local efforts to shape action will be forthcoming from local officials. In a socially homogeneous, small community, it takes great psychic motivation to break out of the mold of acquiescence and conformity with the decisions of dominant local elites; starting a lawsuit or other movement to force change in a policy preferred by the local majority may cause social isolation or even ostracism, and it would not be lightly undertaken. In Midway, it appears, the context was so forbidding that no individual felt it worth the cost to seek to compel compliance with the Court's rulings.

*The Interests, Priorities, Preferences, and Behavior of*
*Political Actors*

State and local public officials and other power holders in the policy context are engaged in a continuing interaction process; they have varying goals and aspirations, and differing capabilities with which to attain them. The only thing that is certain about their relationship is that it has been going on for some time and will continue long after any particular policy is integrated into their political context. Although the least predictable and definable of these four factors, the value-based actions of officials and leaders nevertheless may be the most determinative of ultimate policy. We have seen that officials at all levels operated with a personal cost-benefit equation, seeking only those goals which they valued most highly and sacrificing others. The actions of others might have raised school prayers to a sufficiently public level that action would have *had* to be taken; but since this did not happen, the officials were able to go on about their business unaffected by the 1962 and 1963 Court rulings. In this context, there was little to be gained by action and potentially much to be risked for practically all political actors, whether state or local, and whether official or private. Nobody stood to gain in self-interest by furthering the Court's policy, and so nobody acted. If there had been some important payoff for some power holder in Midway, the whole story might well have been different.

In seeking to understand why a particular policy results in certain specific consequences, all four types of factors must be considered. Ultimate consequences are the product of a complex equation of structures and behavior, and not of any single factor. On occasion, a property of a decision might be highly determinative; at other times less so. Or the role of local decision-makers might vary from case to case. We do not suggest constant importance for each factor relative to all others. But at least all of the factors we have identified as operative here are involved in practically every instance where national policy filters down toward local application, and perhaps many more not apparent from our investigation are also involved. In this inquiry we saw that a constitutional interpretation implying substantial change was cast adrift with very little institutional support available to induce compliance. State and local officials and other elites had no self-interest in furthering it and consequently did nothing. Moreover, both the general context of public attitudes and the specific context of small-town homogeneity discouraged any movement toward compliance. Not surprisingly, the net result was perpetuation of the status quo—even though it meant noncompliance with the law of the land.

Other research into the impact of judicial decisions also emphasizes the tenacity of the status quo. The early work of Patric and Sorauf firmly established that nonuniform responses were the rule rather than the exception in the schoolhouse religion area. Wasby's studies of the impact of obscenity decisions confirmed this finding in that area, and several subsequent studies have done the same in an increasing variety of arenas. Some researchers have emphasized the importance of the interpretation of the law and the language of Court opinions, but none has failed to attribute the wide variability of local response to aspects of the local political context. Birkby assigned some weight to community or school board characteristics; Johnson focused on the values and priorities of the key local actor, the school superintendent; Muir concentrated on the interpersonal relations of individuals in a single school system.[1]

Compliance, it appears, requires some decisive trigger: it can be clear cues from state enforcement authorities, strong determination on the part of key local actors (superintendents, principals, school board members, mayors, school attorneys, or others in authority), or thick-skinned commitment on the part of local citizens (defendants in criminal cases, parents, or taxpayers.) Without such a trigger, however, local authorities, acting to avoid controversy and to preserve as much of the status quo as possible, will normally succeed in insulating the community against the change required by the Court's ruling. But whether or not the nation moves in the direction of compliance, the result normally will be a wide range of outcomes.

### National Issues and Local Responses
### The Relevance for Community Power Studies

We are reasonably confident that persons with power to make educational decisions in the communities we investigated were properly identified. These are towns, after all, not large cities, and we were able to interview many of their involved citizens and hear testimony about many we did not interview. Moreover, the terms we have used to describe these persons—power structure, elite, and so forth—suggest a rather monolithic portrait of the way power is wielded in these settings. But we must also introduce some qualifying considerations.

First, the elites we identified are, as far as we *know,* on top only of educational affairs. Of course, many of the issues in the educational arena involve taxes, bonding, buying and selling property, etc., so it should not be surprising to find that many of the school elites are also elites in other arenas as well. Furthermore, there is a sense in which educational issues in small towns dominate the entire political scene. But there are other crucial political issues, even in the smallest of these Midway communities, and they may involve personnel we neither interviewed nor even heard about. For example, four of the five towns are county seats. Yet we picked up only one tangential comment in one locale that county politics

1. The studies referred to in this paragraph are cited in footnote 5, chapter 1.

intersected or overlapped school politics. That came when Superintendent A. admitted that the Democratic county chairman would "probably be happy to see me go."

Highways are being built through or near these communities; two have recently constructed airports; two have undertaken major programs to attract sportsmen-tourists through the creation of artificial lakes; and one has seen its major economic base, mining, dwindle over a two-decade period. Each of these events means that money goes into or comes out of persons' pockets, and it is unthinkable that politics would fail to enter into deliberations about them. And obviously the state and nation also engage in politics which touch the lives of people in these five communities. Yet we detected very little if any evidence that a school political issue such as prayers and Bible reading got caught in these webs of interests as it got caught in the web of consolidation and school building.

On the basis of the present evidence, therefore, we choose not to take a stand in social scientists' ongoing debate about who generally rules in community politics, but rather to suggest that on some matters there may be little practical difference between an elite and a pluralist position. Put another way, we would ask not *which* but *how* each position is correct.[2]

We observed educational elites in each community. These elites exercised power both in decision making and in setting the agenda. That is to say, not only did a few persons alone decide the outcomes in educational debates but also they had much to do with what issues got debated. The "mobilization of bias," to use Schattschneider's phrase,[3] operated in these communities to keep power fairly well confined to a few.

Let us suppose, however, that as Dahl did in New Haven,[4] we had sought to define decision-making elites on a number of different issues, not just educational affairs but also (for example) the attraction of industry, national-party affairs,

2. An early expression of this possible harmony is Peter Bachrach and Morton S. Baratz, "Two Faces of Power, *"American Political Science Review* 56 (1962): 947–52. More recently William Gamson, *Power and Discontent* (Homewood, Ill.: Dorsey, 1969), has shown how the two positions can be articulated.

3. E. E. Schattschneider, *The Semi-Sovereign People* (New York: Holt, Rinehart & Winston, 1960), p. 71.

4. Robert Dahl, *Who Governs?* (New Haven, Conn.: Yale University Press, 1961).

the building of a new hospital, and the mayoralty campaign. But let us suppose further that the closer we came to decision making in each of these areas, the more we found the same people being interviewed. At the peak of power, perhaps, are a handful of men, all of whom know each other, mix with each other formally and informally, and consult one another on all important issues.

The power structure in this instance might resemble a pyramid, therefore, with each face of the structure representing an issue area, but constructed in such a manner that the higher one climbs on any face, the closer one comes to the same handful of men. At the bottom of each face are persons who may not know their counterparts on other faces, but nearer the top are those who do know who are on the other faces until finally, at the top, is a small coterie deciding all the issues. The elite for each issue-area would be the same for all issues.

Such a portrait, we think, is not inaccurate for the two smallest communities we investigated (even though we would want more evidence for that assertion). In the two towns of 10,000 population it would appear to be a somewhat less accurate portrait; and in the one city of 45,000, less accurate still. Tentatively, then, population size might seem to be related to the shape taken by community power: a single pyramid in small towns, multiple pyramids in larger cities. Put in different terms, with increased population size comes increased population heterogeneity, thus increased heterogeneity of power bases from which to make the ascent to a pyramid top.[5]

However, with population heterogeneity comes an increase in the heterogeneity of both "faces of power"— decision-making and agenda-setting. Pluralism, where it exists, exists not simply in the sense that various interest groups share in deciding final outcomes; pluralism can also exist in the sense of providing multiple channels to varieties of people who would help set the agenda. The "values, the myths, and the

5. See Michael Aiken, "The Distribution of Community Power: Structural Bases and Social Consequences," in Michael Aiken and Paul E. Mott, eds., *The Structure of Community Power:* (New York: Random House, 1970). Aiken, using fifty-seven case studies, demonstrates a positive relationship between community size and pluralization of power and attributes this relationship to "structural differentiation" or heterogeneity.

established political procedures and rules of the game,"[6] in other words, also become more open.

If this proposition is correct, then several facts observed in this research become explicable. First, the Midway communities found to be complying (though we did not interview there) were Midway's large capital city and several of its university cities. Second, the national resurvey in 1967 of Dierenfield's 1960 sample of school districts found compliance to be positively related to population size. And third, the same resurvey found compliance also to be positively related to the percentage of "foreign stock" in the community.[7] The common element in these three situations is the presumed presence of multiple bases of power—through size, ethnic organization, or the presence of a university—and the implication is that the dissident minority will find it easier to challenge the public school status quo when multiple bases of power are present.

The discussion in the previous chapter on the impotence of nonelites can now be recalled with a new understanding. Given the small size and ethnic homogeneity of the communities investigated, those few persons who might have set in motion the process whereby schools would abolish prayers and Bible reading were unable to do so in the absence of any power base other than that which ran the schools. Such dissidents had neither effective threats to make nor representatives of their own power base who could negotiate with the educational elite. The small, homogeneous town operates its schools in a manner which closely reflects the desires of its homogeneous citizenry, at the cost of a structured inattentiveness to the few citizens not falling into the single mold.[8]

Generalized further our research findings would suggest that whatever democracy the large, bureaucratic, impersonal,

6. Bachrach and Baratz, "Two Faces of Power," p. 952.

7. See above, p. 32 for a description of Dierenfield's survey and Appendix for a description of the resurvey. The findings just cited, incidentally, are based on only the Midwest—those states, it will be remembered, where local rather than state action on school prayers was most relevant. The findings, then, are not an artifact of wholesale compliance in populous, ethnically mixed New England and wholesale noncompliance in rural, native American southern states.

8. See Sorauf, "Zorach v. Clauson," p. 791, for another illustration of this point in the context of a church-state issue.

delegated system loses by way of reduced citizen participation and by distant decision making, it gains by way of an increased attentiveness to minority interests channeled through its multiple power bases. Cast in more human terms, and in the present context, the lone atheist, or Jew, or committed Supreme Court devotee, if he lives in a small town, may find the school system closer to him geographically but not politically when the issue puts him at odds with the large majority. Located in a larger city, such a person, though finding the school system more distant, at least will have structured channels for getting his complaints considered. Put in the terms of social status, the smaller or more homogeneous the population, the more overlap will there be among those at the top of the status structures and/or power issues. Thus the relative homogeneity of those in control serves both to minimize participation in decision making and to constrict the power to determine agendas. Both faces of power in other words, are more elitist than pluralist under conditions of population homogeneity.

This is not to say, of course, that small towns play small politics in small ways. Clearly the case cannot be so simply put; centralized power, to the degree it accompanies small size, does so in a subtle as well as a blatant manner. Thus for example, schoolhouse religion, as a style issue, provided local elites with considerable room for discretion, as we observed in the previous chapter. Note, however, that the *style* nature of the issue meant fewer channels for public expression of its political will, but that fact also meant a greater flexibility for elites to get involved or not. That the local elites we observed should choose not to get involved in schoolhouse religion ought to surprise no one, of course, but the structural importance of their choice needs to be accented. Where elite rather than pluralist control might more commonly be found in smaller communities, therefore, so also might it more commonly be found surrounding *style* rather than *economic* issues. The latter, we would estimate, even in small towns is more often based on continuing relationships, thus permitting less flexibility to the relevant elites. Their commitment—their activity—is less predetermined, so to speak, by a style issue. They can, alone, more easily control a style issue's destiny.

We bring this matter up only to show how both elitist and pluralist positions may be correct but differentially reflecting reality depending not only on population complexity but also on the nature of the issue. The rather deliberate inaction of Midway's elites was not simply a matter of disinterest, then, but in part a calculated maneuver made possible by both of these factors. Had we investigated an economic, rather than a style issue, and had we done so in metropolitan, not small town, Midway, no doubt a pluralist flavor would more likely have entered our discussions in this book.

One other point might be made before leaving this matter of community power. It is not only possible but inevitable that people will exercise power without necessarily knowing they do so. That is to say, much determination of our social behavior comes from the actions of others who neither know nor care that they influence us. Frequently these instances are trivial in outcome and thus may be theoretically trivial as well, but that is not always the case. The power to "set the agenda," the "mobilization of bias," the "second face of power"—these represent efforts to control nontrivial instances where influence is felt, however subtly it is exercised.

Such subtle power can be explained, however, even if the intentions of those involved are quite unrelated to the outcomes. Unintended consequences are no less caused for being unintended. This has been one of the major understandings emerging from the civil rights battle—that "institutional racism," in settings where nobody is "prejudiced," is nevertheless productive of the same consequences as would be produced by prejudiced persons. Forces can be subtle and unintended, but they are still powerful.

Now it is significant that awareness of institutional racism came with the popularity of the term *power structure,* that institutionalized arrangement whereby agendas are set and decisions rendered. For until the power to determine the agenda was seen, until the established procedures were observed to admit some issues and deny others, the full sense in which power is structured was not seen either. Thus, one need not believe exclusively in conspiracies in order to see how elites can predetermine as well as determine outcomes. And neither must one believe only in righteous motives to see how outcomes can be pluralistically determined. What one must see, however, is that outcomes result not simply from who wins what issues but also from whether they ever become issues. Thus, de facto segregation in northern school districts, to use an obvious example, was not even recognized as a political issue, a proper item on a community's agenda, until it was in some measure seen as institutionalized racism.

In effect, much of the inertia we saw in Midway over school prayers might be attributed in the analogous sense to "institutionalized religiosity," but it is nonetheless political for being that. The structures permitting what we called "the conflict-avoidance ethic" and "the impotence of the little man" just as surely had their consequences for maintaining a religious status quo, even if it turns out that the elites in those structures were hardly interested.

### Generalizing about Processes of Change

Many interesting case studes of the reception of Supreme Court cases remain to be done. When they are, it may be possible to develop more precise and complete theories of the impact of judicial decisions. A substantial research investment will be needed, however, to bridge the gap between investigations so general and abstract as to border on the self-evident, and the excessively particularized accounts needed to describe the variety of possibilities in all subject areas of the Court's decision-making activity. A somewhat similar condition obtains in the field of community power studies: an important new setting for political activity has been researched in ways that have contributed significantly to the understanding of politics, but a comprehensive theory is still far off.

At the conclusion of a study which touched upon both of these fields, it seems to us that each might stand to gain from more frequent intersection. Our problem was to understand the ways in which change comes about or is prevented in the American political system; our focus was on local community reception of an innovative Supreme Court decision. In order to gain the understanding we sought, we were obliged to draw on both fields, selecting findings and interpretations from each which were relevant to the larger problem. To us, this has meant that the boundaries between research subareas had to be broken and each field mined for what was instructive in regard to one of the great questions of social science—the nature of the process of social and political change. We think that this is not only likely to bring the results of research in each field closer to the kind of social relevance that today's domestic problems demand, but also can contribute to the development of each subfield's more parochial needs for definition and theory.

In our view, integration of several compartments and sub-fields of research through focusing on major problems is now in order, at least in the areas touched upon in this study. Although our data do not permit carrying this effort very far, we do think that we have developed enough evidence to allow informed speculation in several directions. We shall suggest some in the paragraphs that follow.

Are the four categories into which we organized our findings about factors influencing reception of Supreme Court decisions limited to the circumstances of the Supreme Court's outlawing of school prayers, or do they extend to other Supreme Court rulings and perhaps to the acts of other policy-making institutions as well? We examined only the one situation, of course, and have evidence only on what transpired in response to two Court rulings in the schoolhouse religion area. All else is speculation, but it still seems that our findings lead to some sketchy implications of a more general nature. Regarding Court decisions, it appears that the capacity of subsequent actors to alter the outcome is greatest when the new policy requires substantial change in the behavior patterns of numbers of people in an area where official enforcement depends on local residents' invocation of the courts. The more clearly the obligation to respond is focused upon a few identifiable public officials, and the more available are enforcement agencies (such as the Civil Rights Division of the Justice Department, or criminal courts in the case of defendants' rights issues), the more limited is the range of discretion on the part of post–policy-making forces and people. There is always some discretion on the part of political actors subsequent to any Court decision, of course, and the variation is only in the degree to which a given ruling is subject to the manipulations of others. In most cases, it seems safe to say, a large share of the shaping of ultimate results rests with political actors on the local level, rather than with the higher courts' views of the merits of issues.

Perhaps this is a point at which our findings show even greater generality. The extent of local capacity to shape policy consequences appears in important ways to be a reflection of the national institution that created the particular policy. A policy produced by the Supreme Court is probably much more open to discretionary implementation by a variety of domestic political forces than is a congressional statute or an executive regulation. The availability of detailed clarifying and implementing instructions, or a bureaucracy with oversight and persuasion capabilities, to say nothing of the inherent legal capacity to bind all persons with a single pronouncement, cannot help but reduce the opportunity for local forces to shape implementation and ultimate consequences. It does not prevent such forces from exercising power or from affecting the outcome, of course, but their opportunities are more restricted. In contrast with Court-produced policies, which depend on volunteered cooperation or a sense of obligation on the part of state and local officials, congressional and executive actions have a ready-made corps of federal implementors waiting to convert policy into consequences.

Recognition of greater enforcement capabilities in the nonjudicial institutions should not lead to hasty conclusions about their absolute capabilities for effecting change. Examples from Prohibition to civil rights are too readily available to permit such a leap. Local political cultures and the cost-benefit context for local officials are still powerful shaping factors. In short, our categories appear to encompass much of what common experience tells us are the actual consequences of much legislation requiring change in broad segments of the general public. If more empirical studies of actual consequences had been done, of course, we could test our categories in a much more satisfying manner.

Let us try an even broader approach from such an integrated, problem-centered start. What have we learned about American politics from the study of the consequences of these Supreme Court decisions? By extension, what might we learn from the study of the consequences of national policies generally? Clearly, we have much to gain in the way of new understanding about how things actually work in politics—about how great a gap may exist between official interpretation of the Constitution and actual practice, for example, and how that gap happens to come about. We may also be able to come to grips with the elusive problem of change: when is change accomplished, when not, and why is it possible in some circumstances and not in others? Finally, we may gain a new basis for evaluation of the American political system, specifically how well it is working in terms of its basic values, its problem-solving capacities, or its democratic qualities. Let us take up each of these possibilities in order.

### Understanding Noncompliance

Throughout this book, we have seen evidence converging to form four major explanations for the substantial gap between official constitutional interpretation and actual local practice in Midway. First, we saw that all state and local power holders—both official and private—had what seemed to them good reasons for not taking the actions and suffering the probable costs necessary to carry out the Court's mandates. Given their priorities and their perceptions of their political contexts, it was simply not worth the trouble. And so they used the discretion inherent in the ambiguities of the decisions and enforcement structure to do nothing. Second, we saw that this inertia was rationalized in at least two major ways: by "misunderstanding" the requirements of the Court rulings so as to permit teacher discretion, and by resisting knowledge about the extent and character of prayers and other religious observances in the schools. This tendency was noticeable at all levels and was apparently unconscious; only a few persons frankly confessed both knowledge and impotency, and only one acknowledged his somewhat cynical personal encouragement of religious observances despite recognizedly conflicting official obligations. Third, we saw that local elites were not so much against the Court or the decisions as they were wary of conflict in their communities. The effect of this latter concern was the perpetuation of the unconstitutional practices in their schools, of course, but they were untroubled by that. Fourth, we saw that there were no institutional channels through which local citizens could effectively activate the rulings.

These are not the exclusive explanations for the noncompliance found in Midway, for there are many interwoven strands which produced that result. But identification of even these modest themes is an advance over blithely ascribing noncompliant response in one instance to public opposition and compliant response in another to public approval. The fact is that compliance is not an either/or situation but rather a wide range of actions, a *process* of continuing response and adjustment. Thus we have preferred to speak of consequences and responses and to look at the extent and nature of discretionary shaping of such results by power holders at the state and local level. In so doing, we have focused on a segment of the political process not often explored by scholars and perhaps not highly obvious to laymen. This postdecision or post–policy-making process is instrumental, however, in determining what actually happens to people—and that is what is most crucial about politics. By exploring who does what to shape the actual final results of government action, we can hope to complete our knowledge of who gets what, when, and how through political activity. From what we have seen here, we must realize that very little may really be decided by the words of a decision or a statute; the enunciation of such national policy may be just the beginning of the decisive process of determining what will happen to whom, and understanding this further stage is essential to a full understanding of politics.

**The Process of Change**
It has been difficult to analyze the complex processes involved in social and political change precisely enough to know what conditions or actions promote or prevent change. But one way to approach this problem is to focus on different patterns of policy consequences—in situations where a government action causes people to change their behavior, and in those where it does not. In this study, we have found several reasons why change did not occur in Midway in the direction mandated by national policy. We also saw how Midway was different from other settings in which such change did occur, and we can therefore speculate about the process of change with more evidence than before. For example, it seems clear that greater exposure of the actions of state officials in this subject area would have increased opportunities for them to support the Court's rulings. A more focused decision which assigned responsibility for enforcement would also have contributed to compliance, as would a more vigorous public effort on the part of sympathetic interest-group leaders and their organizations. Establishing means for taxpayers or citizens to bring lawsuits to enforce minority rights such as those at stake here would also put more pressure on state officials: somewhere within a state there will probably always be somebody willing to litigate over failure to take action in support of minority rights, and state officials could not afford to ignore new constitutional

interpretations quite so readily. To take another example, we saw that local elites were more concerned with preventing controversy than they were concerned with the specific merits of the schools-prayers issue. Finding ways to 'threaten them with the prospect of controversy unless they acted to enforce the Court's decisions might therefore have been sufficient to bring them down on the other side of the fence. If local elites acted to rid the schools of religious observances, the decision would probably be accepted by the local public, and in any event it would eventually be sustained in the courts.

If this view seemed valid, the Supreme Court (or perhaps any decision-making body) might create procedures making it easier for unrepresented persons to make complaints known. Especially in matters of style, where structured interest groups are less common than in economic matters, devices might be instituted to facilitate the channeling of complaints. At higher levels the need is less, perhaps, because of the plethora of organizations interested in style issues (for example, with respect to schoolhouse religion, such organizations as the American Civil Liberties Union or the Anti-Defamation League). The failure of these associations was, as pointed out above, at the state level, in their neglect to hear local complaints or to initiate action with state officials. But at lawer levels, the relative scarcity of style deviants means that structured channels enabling their views to be known are also scarce. Thus, no local CLU or ADL chapter existed in any of the communities we studied; even had a rare person objected to continuing school religious practices, he would have had great difficulty manifesting his objection.

The second illustration of insight gained into the process of change through this study emerges from our findings that whereas school prayers were a great national issue, in Midway they were a matter of no local conflict whatsoever. The contrast we found between nation-wide attentiveness to Court actions, the campaign to amend the Constitution to permit prayers, and other national manifestations of the issue, on the one hand, and the lack of both knowledge and controversy at the local level, on the other, suggests that there is a major disjunction between national and local affairs. Perhaps there are separate publics for the two levels of issues. If so, resourceful persons desiring change might make use of specific local situations in order to focus the efforts of supporters of the national policy. But possibly even those who consider national policy important and find satisfaction in working to achieve change at that rather abstract level are reluctant to undergo the personal costs of accomplishing the same goals in their local contexts. If true, this may go a long way toward explaining why change in actual practices is often so hard to achieve, and it may help to explain why images of change abound while the status quo, in terms of the reality of people's lives, endures.

Indeed, the fact of noncompliance is so eminently understandable in the light of our findings that it may well be asked why any rational person should have expected local people to act consistently with the Court's rulings in the first place. We found a kind of banality of noncompliance—a series of homely, everyday circumstances and decisions that led local officials and elites to ignore the Court and continue about their business. No great principles were perceived to be at stake. It was merely a case of all power holders independently concluding that their responsibilities did not include the costly task of upholding the law of the land. Ironically, the same elites would probably be among those who would call most loudly for obedience to law and order in the cities and for the suppression of violations of the rights of others in such settings as college campuses. But their own transcendence of minority constitutional rights is so commonplace and so unexceptional that it scarcely deserves special recognition. In concrete settings, of course, the law is very much a question of whose ox is being gored, and this case study shows clearly that "respectable" people are in an excellent position to ignore or use the law for their own ends on a regular basis. If and when others seek to do so, it is a matter to be deplored; but under the proper circumstances of elite management, the law may be conveniently fitted to the needs of office holders and other regular political participants.

## Evaluation of the Workings of the Political System

How is an operating political system to be evaluated? One might not unreasonably ask to what extent it succeeds in realizing its declared values. One of these values in America clearly is the separation of church and state, with resulting endorsement of religious pluralism. The Supreme Court asserted such values as crucial factors in these decisions. Yet, as we pointed out, the separation of church and state has two distinct, but sometimes contradictory, meanings: free exercise and nonestablishment. Ironically, almost everyone who might disagree with the Court on *Engel* v. *Vitale* or *Schempp* would justify his disagreement with a free-exercise argument. Thus, as muckrakers of an earlier day and functionalist-oriented social scientists of the present day are wont to point out, pursuit of one value is likely to inhibit the furtherance of another value. In this case, a Supreme Court decision to uphold a nonestablishment interpretation of the First Amendment goal has had the effect of activating the free-exercise interpretation, leading to an inhibition of the aims implicit in nonestablishment.

Another value standard might be the system's capacity to solve internal tensions with some degree of timeliness and justice. Judgment in this respect probably depends more on one's definition of the nature of the problem than on specification of the events that transpired. There was no problem in Midway before the Court ruled school prayers unconstitutional, but there probably were people who, after the decision, would have liked to have had their newly declared constitutional rights observed. The policy-implementing process we have examined apparently lacked the capacity to carry out their wishes, however, and to that extent minority rights were sacrificed. But perhaps one should be more concerned with the capacity of majorities to delay changes of which they disapproved. If it could be shown that the actions of officials and local elites were indeed taken in the name of majority preference, there might be a kind of inherent stability to celebrate in the system. But the question of whether long-run stability is served by permitting majorities to deny minorities their official constitutional rights would still remain.

These concluding remarks suggest the utility of exploring the consequences of national policies, not only for the understanding of how the political system works, but also for the purpose of assessing the process of change and for reaching evaluations about how well it is working. One relatively narrow study of how and why the responsible authorities and local elites of a single state could justify continued noncompliance with a constitutional interpretation by the nation's highest court can only be suggestive of the potential in such inquiry. But it does constitute a warning that we should not take the passage of statutes or the enunciation of national policy in other forms as being anything more than the opening of a long struggle in which lower level power holders often have the last word. And perhaps it suggests that other such studies would show an even greater gap between statutory rhetoric and empirical reality in other areas of government action.

# Appendix     Research Note

We have had access, in the course of writing this book, to
a variety of data. Most of our information, of course, came
through interviews conducted in Midway by the two of us
or by graduate student assistants. But, since the study
represents the culmination of several years of collaboration,
during which several component projects were completed
under our direction, we shall take these final pages to identify
the full range of information sources available to us.

In the spring of 1966 the Wisconsin Survey Research
Laboratory included in its survey of an area probability
sample of 600 Wisconsin adults a handful of questions
about the United States Supreme Court. These questions
provided measures of the public's level of information about
and evaluation of the Court. Three months later, mail
questionnaires, asking the same questions, were sent by
two graduate students to three types of Wisconsin leaders:
county chairmen of the two political parties, clergymen,
and newspaper editors. In 1968 Eleanor Perlmutter completed an M.A. thesis, "Leader-Non-Leader Differences in
Benevolence toward the Supreme Court," which was based

on some of these findings. Some of those comparisons are
referred to in chapter 2 above.

During this same period, we analyzed all of the survey
data on file with the Roper Center for Public Opinion Research (plus some other surveys to which we had access)
which dealt with the public's evaluation of the Court as an
institution. This analysis was published in 1968.[1] Two of
these surveys permitted the Texas-Minnesota comparison
cited in chapter 2, and two others led to another M.A. thesis
in sociology—this one by Carolyn Shettle in 1967—"An
Analysis of Public Opinion on the Supreme Court Prayer
Decision Cases," cited in chapters 4 and 5.

In spring of 1967, Professor R. B. Dierenfield of Macalester College kindly allowed us to use his 1960 survey
of religious practices in American public schools. As noted
in the text, his return rate from school superintendents was
slightly more than 50 percent, of which about half were
engaged in 1960 in practices that three years later were
declared unconstitutional. During summer 1967 we resurveyed all 1150 of these latter school districts, receiving only
a slightly higher return rate (57 percent) with our postcard
questionnaire. Our estimates of compliance, reported in chapter 3, are drawn from the resurvey, though, as noted in that
chapter, our estimates conform remarkably well to those
gained by other surveys. A law student, Eric Schulenberg,
meanwhile, was collating the public pronouncements and
acts, state by state, or legislatures, lower courts, attorneys
general, and state superintendents of education. The outcome,
shown in a table in chapter 3, helped us decide to focus
on a Midwestern state (not Wisconsin) in which no state-
level action had occurred.

Early in 1968 the Walter E. Meyer Institute of Law
granted us funds to support a number of interviewing trips
to Midway. Selecting initially four small cities on which we
planned to concentrate, we sent a graduate student first to
interview the daily newspaper editors and note any news
stories about schoolhouse religion appearing after June 1962,
when *Engel* v. *Vitale* was announced. Because he uncovered
no evidence of community concern over this issue, and because in interviews with school superintendents the next

1. Dolbeare and Hammond, "The Political Party Basis . . .", pp.
16–30.

month, we also found no evidence of such concern, we subsequently added a fifth, larger city and sought interviews with state officials, both governmental and private. All together we conducted over 150 interviews, from officials in the Attorney General's Office to elementary school teachers, from the president of the Midway Civil Liberties Union to local school board members, from heads of local Chambers of Commerce to newspaper reporters. In addition, we gathered any written documents, from the statewide survey of religious practices to telephone books, which we thought might provide clues to decision-making in these communities. Interviewers were instructed to keep alert to hints of who held power and how it was wielded.

All informants were assured anonymity, of course, and this is why it was necessary here to employ the awkward pseudonym "Midway." Tape recorders were used, but only for paraphrased recounting of conversations which had just occurred. The candor of almost all interviewees not only convinced us of the authenticity of their remarks but also provided us with a major theme of this report: ,no one had anything to hide because hardly anyone judged that his community was doing anything illegal. The transposing of an establishment issue into a free-exercise issue was nearly complete.

Our prior work on public attitudes toward the Supreme Court, and the contrasting knowledge levels of leaders and nonleaders regarding Court activity, found ready confirmation in the field work in these communities. It was clear from the beginning that local elites knew more of what was going on in the schoolhouse religion area, and given the freedom granted them by the inactivity at the state level, it became clear that these same local elites ultimately shaped the decisions to accord with their own desires. How and why that shaping took place became the theme of this book.

# Index